Di

Dirty Days

Born to be a Miner

Pete McGowan

Originally published by the author 2019;
this revised edition published in 2020.

Originally published in Great Britain by Pete McGowan,

mcgowanpete@hotmail.co.uk

http://www.wilfsincredibleprank.co.uk/

ISBN 978-1-9162081-0-0

A catalogue record of this book is available from the British Library.

Printed by Book Empire.

The wind howls as it tears its way, maliciously spitting sleet, battering the rooftops and pavements of the grey streets of the estate, litter is tossed in the air when dustbins spill their intestines, and there stray dogs enjoy their oysters

Milk bottles rattle and gates clank as the dwellers slumber peacefully inside, still riding the dream waves in their posturized chariots, until the ecstasy of deep sleep reaches its peak

Suddenly the night is pierced by a chorus of alarm clocks, sounds of every description, erupting as if spontaneous, with the pit siren harmonising in the distance, calling out to the men from the mine, momentarily fading as the fierce wind carries its unwelcome beckoning away

New lights begin to ignite, illuminating households, shortly followed by the sounds of thumping doors, as once burning lights are now extinguished, dark figures now shrug their way down garden paths, grumbling uttering words of distaste, nervous sparrows flutter under gutters, prematurely awoke from deep sleep, by the crank of car engines and the vrumming of buses hurrying through the streets, nervous cats dart into their flaps, while the unlucky rat sets off a well oiled trap, and the lowly dog continues to bark only until the mortal noise gets swallowed into the distant dark

And just as the night regains its rhythm, a second siren sounds, announcing the start of another day shift, and while a young child nestles deep into its pillow safe and sound, a father descends deeper and deeper, into the ground...

By Pete McGowan 1984

Glossary

in-bye: means towards the workings and coal face.

out-bye: means away from the workings and the way out of the mine.

It was in 1975 when I officially left school, in reality I opted out of education a year earlier and to be truthful my attendance at a certain catholic comprehensive went into a steady decline from day one, but that's another long story!

So I left school with little or no qualifications at all and it was no surprise then that the only jobs available to me were in labouring types of work, which I didn't mind because as I was never shy of hard graft and anyhow seeing as most of Britain's industry was still heavily labour intensive I didn't feel there was any shame in doing a man's job.

I was desperate for work our family was poor and we lived on the bread line for a number of years, and the reason was due to my Dad returning home from the Second World War damaged! Originally he was a coal miner at the local St John's colliery where he was a pony driver underground, but he hated it because he was an intelligent man and he should have gone on to better things, he also thought the use of ponies down the mine was very cruel. In my infant days I remember him taking us to see the pit ponies on the day they were allowed to come out of the mine once a year for a short period of time in the colliery's annual holidays. It was a great spectacle to witness, it used to draw quite a crowd of people too, who like us were all there waiting to see the pit ponies as they came out into the daylight and released into the field for first time and share in their happiness as they excitedly bounced and buckaroo'd with joy at their new found freedom in the open air. I have a particularly vivid memory of that day because my Dad sat me on the top of the fence bar for a better view, and the while he was holding my hand for reassurance I remembered his words at the time, which must have impacted on me when he said, "it was a really nice thing to see but it was still very sad all the same", and when he did I noticed his eyes were slightly filling with water, bless him.

So in desperation to get out the mines my Dad seized the opportunity when WW2 came along and went straight to a recruiting office where he even lied about his age to join the King's own Yorkshire light infantry, who were more commonly referred to as the KOYLI'S Regiment in those days, but they questioned his age. Still determined to join up he made the extra effort by travelling to the north of England in the company of a Jewish man who shared the same predicament of being too young, where they both eventually managed to join the Royal Artillery Regiment there.

The only reason he got his job at the local colliery in the first place was because of an incident that happened one day nearing the end of his final year of education. He and a couple of his mates were out nesting for bird's eggs in a place that is locally known as the Carriage drive in the Newland area of Normanton which was the private road to an old estate that was then occupied by the colliery owner at that time. This particular afternoon my Dad and his mates were rooting about in the hedgerows of this carriage drive when they were confronted by the coal owners son who was on horseback. According to my Dad his manner towards them was very much like the Flashman character from the *Tom Brown's School Days* novel and film, because he was so arrogant and high handed towards them, even threatening them with prosecution! In retaliation to his attitude my Dad and his mates gave him some good old fashioned working class lip in return, which was a bit too Bolshy for this coal owner's son (The Bolshevik Revolution in Russia was only in 1917 and it worried the upper classes it could happen here, and common people answering back to the ruling classes were usually labelled as Bolshy) who took it upon himself to administer my

Dad a dammed good thrashing by lashing him with his riding crop.

Upon hearing of this incident my Granddad who was a central figure in the Irish community that used to settle new migrants from his old country and get them lodgings and work and such like, was having none of this, and at risk of losing his own job he immediately went to the coal mine and confronted the colliery owner about his son's behaviour. He was a proud man and wouldn't accept this treatment from anyone; he marched straight into his office, not cap in hand either and demanded something be done about it! Surprisingly the colliery owner agreed with my Granddad and said he would do something about it and apologised for his son's brash behaviour.

However on my Granddad leaving the office the colliery owner said, "Tell your son Hughie that when he leaves school at the end of term I expect to see him here the first Monday in the month to start work" and despite being a clever lad this is how he got his job down the mine. Although he had passed his 11 plus to go to grammar school his parents were told by the local authorities it was beyond his family's reach both financially and socially, which ultimately robbed him of higher education.

Eventually after completing his army induction he was sent to North Africa with his regiment in the Eighth Army to acclimatise there before landing at Salerno in the Italian campaign (Here's another great story, but to be told another time) from Salerno he went on to Monte Casino where he was in charge of taking heavy armour to the front, and it was around this time he had made the rank of sergeant. Unfortunately a short time later he got blown up when the forward compound he was stationed in was attacked by a SS rear Mortar brigade, as a consequence he was hospitalised suffering from concussion, broken ribs and a broken jaw that clicked every time he ate his food. Surprisingly on his return home he threw himself straight into the boxing ring after learning the skill in the army, to eventually become a professional light heavy weight boxer, however he only had a short career of three professional bouts and retired after getting knocked out by a boxer from the USA. It wasn't too long after this he began to have different bouts, but not in a ring, these were severe bouts of depression. My Dad was an honourable man and he couldn't face life with depression, so he sought help by putting his trust in doctors who foolishly convinced him he should have electric shock therapy, and later when that didn't work they then talked him into having two partial frontal lobotomies. So it was no surprise that by the time they had finished with him they had left us with a dad who had regular seizures and fits, and dependent of a cocktail of drugs which made him incapable of fetching home the bacon for his family for a number of years.

The boom of the sixties never reached our house, in the seventies we were still living in the fifties.

It was only a couple of years ago that my brother told me why the two of us sometimes used to get a cold reception from certain mates' parents when we visited their house, it really shocked me to find out what this mates had told him, he said his dad thought my dad was a malingerer and some people in the community were of the opinion that my Dad should have acted like a man and gone to work! But these people who made these comments had never been to war, so I can slightly understand their ignorance, but still it was very unfair!

So yes, I reckon I was fed up of being skint all the time and I just wanted to get a job and earn some money for a change. I did actually pass a few entrance exams for apprenticeships but I didn't fancy going back to school for six months, that would be like going to prison to me. So it was just a case of waiting for my application to go through at the local colliery to start work there just like everyone else.

It was common knowledge at the time that if an applicant added the numbers of his family already working in the mining industry to his application form the more points he got in favour over other applicants, and because I had several relatives in the industry and three of them working at the pit I was applying to I was on to a dead cert and the a job was in the bag, I thought?

When September came around jobs were a plenty for the new school leavers, and week by week I kept hearing news of my mates getting starts at the pit and factories around the area, so after a couple of phone call enquiries to find out if the colliery had indeed received my application, and after been reassured that they had, I waited a while longer still confident I was going to get a start. I patiently waited and waited but September soon became October and it was now becoming a bit obvious that I had been left out of the influx of new starters for this year. It was depressing I couldn't even get a job down the pit!

So I went looking for work wherever I could, but the only vacancies that were available only paid half the wage a miner got. I even considered signing up to join the Army but I soon came to the realisation that I wasn't the sort of person that could conform or liked taking orders.

Then one day I was sitting in the living room feeling miserable and dejected and thinking why me, when my Dad walked in and on noticing my pathetic demeanour he shook his head in disgust and began making sneering comments about my long hair and lacklustre to find a job. As one can imagine the arguments that followed from then on, and no sooner I had exhausted every excuse to defend my case as to why I was still unemployed, and just as I was rounding it off by making the point that there was nothing going that was worth doing, my Dad then took the well timed opportunity to throw the Daily Mirror newspaper onto my lap, which I saw was half folded over and he had encircled an advert on the jobs page in blue biro pen for my attention. It read: AN EXCITING AND WELL PAID CAREER IN DEEP SEA TRAWLERS... blah, blah, blah... Wanted TRAINEE FISHERMEN, then he said "there's an exciting job for you, why don't you go do that".

So trusting the wisdom of a man who had half his brain taken out I went straight to the red phone box at the end of the next street and phoned the number on the advert. Surprisingly I was given an interview date over the phone for the following week and received the official confirmation through the post two days later which informed me to attend a mass recruitment on St Andrew's dock in Hull. Before the interview date had arrived I had checked out the journey time beforehand and it turned out that it was going to take two trains and about three hours to get there, even though it was only 70 mile as the crow flies, none the less I just had to go, I wasn't going to let my dad get the better of me, he threw down the gauntlet and I picked it up. You see...when my Dad got fed up of hearing me moan about not having a job he would say "I should have gone to school instead of skiving off all the time and I wouldn't be in this mess I'm in now", and usually finishing with off with the comment, "I was useless and would never amount to anything" He didn't mean it, it was just his way of using like a reverse psychology, he thought that by saying this I would want to show him different!

So I guessed it worked in a sense?

A Snacker

There I was on a cold foggy mid October Monday morning standing in Hull train station asking strangers the way St Andrew's dock, only then to find it was at least four mile away, and because I couldn't afford a taxi I had no other choice but to go on foot, but I'm glad I did or I would have missed a lot of interesting sights.

On reaching the docks area my first observations was that it smelled very fishy and there was lots of activity. The funny thing was that there were hundreds of people milling about and what they all had in common was that they all wore the same white hats and smocks, leggings, even white Wellies to match! To see the fish being unloaded from the trawlers was also very interesting, which made the walk was a pleasurable one, and before I knew it I had already arrived at my destination. It was a big warehouse on the quayside and there was about two hundred other would be recruit's that were already assembled outside and waiting for the interviews to start.

Eventually we were all let inside to sit in this great hall where we were all told to sit and wait to be called each in turn to a small office at the end of the room to be interviewed. While I was waiting I couldn't resist being my natural chatty self and was more than happy to join a conversation with anyone, so it wasn't long before I was chatting to all the other candidates that were sat in my vicinity. On the other lads first hearing my accent they were amazed to hear that I had actually come all that way from inland to get a job at sea, and they were even more amazed to hear that I hadn't come to get the more cushy jobs in the Galley that were below deck, but I had come for the more dangerous one as a Decky.

On everyone else hearing this news I was immediately surrounded by the other lads that were in my area, who were all eager to tell me their worst sea fairing horror stories, telling me of how many souls were swept overboard each year and reminding me that if a man went overboard and he didn't get out the icy cold waters within five minutes he would be overcome by hypothermia and die.

They also threw in a few other stories of fishermen losing fingers and having to hack ice off the ship as well! Which wasn't making me feel optimistic about my new choice of career at all, and the more they told their tales the thought of committing interview suicide or just leaving the building flashed through my mind a few times I can tell ya!

Though before I could think any more about it or change my mind, it became too late when I heard my name being called out and I was quickly ushered into the interview room at the end of the hall, where on entering I was greeted by these three suited but very weathered faced men who were sat behind this big old office desk. The first thing I noticed was that they seemed to have looks of bemusement written across their faces, it was as though they were mystified by me or perhaps they were trying to figure out if I was nut-job or not. To be honest I reckon someone would have to be a nut-job to want a job of this kind in the first place. None the less they were still happy to see me. After what I consider to be the briefest interview I've ever had they set me on there on the spot, and before I knew it I was then being led by one of these men to the Fishermans mission, where on arrival at this old red brick building he showed me the sleeping quarters for trainee fishermen (trainee fishermen were called Snackers) and where I was told to report to the following Sunday evening.

This salty old sea dog then took me for a short stroll down to the dock quayside where there was a long row of rusty ships all moored inline and at first I didn't have a clue where he was taking me, I was just obediently following from behind, but I couldn't help asking him as to why all these rusty ships were moored there, and hoping to provide him with the right answer, I said was it because they were old ships and they were now destined for the scrap yard?" No sooner I had this sea dog then stopped in dead in his tracks, right next to the biggest rustiest one there and said "No lad, this will be your Ship". On the sight of this ship and hearing this news my heart fell into the pit of my stomach, I've never felt so gutted in all my life, and if things couldn't get any worse they did, when this old salt then enquired as to whether I got sea sick or not? Oh boy oh boy was I dumb, until that very moment I had never considered that at all, but what was even more heart wrenching was the answer to his question, which was yes I did get sea sick.

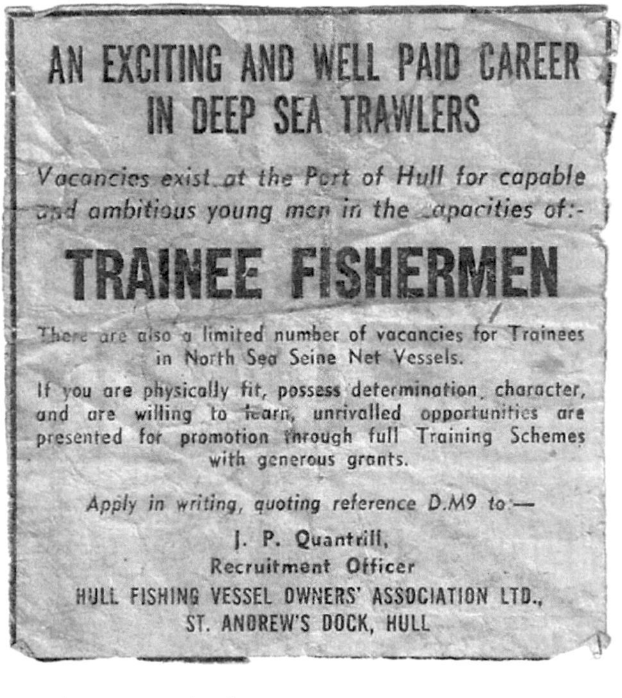
AN EXCITING AND WELL PAID CAREER IN DEEP SEA TRAWLERS

Vacancies exist at the Port of Hull for capable and ambitious young men in the capacities of:-

TRAINEE FISHERMEN

There are also a limited number of vacancies for Trainees in North Sea Seine Net Vessels.

If you are physically fit, possess determination, character, and are willing to learn, unrivalled opportunities are presented for promotion through full Training Schemes with generous grants.

Apply in writing, quoting reference D.M9 to:—

J. P. Quantrill,
Recruitment Officer
HULL FISHING VESSEL OWNERS' ASSOCIATION LTD.,
ST. ANDREW'S DOCK, HULL

The actual newspaper advertisement

Sea fishing trip tale

I was once invited to go on a 6 hour long deep sea wreck fishing trip!

I remember that day very well because it was not only a really funny experience but a weird one at the same time. My mate Col had asked me to join him to give him some younger company because he was going with his three older uncles and it would make it more fun for him if I came along. After agreeing to go the five of us all headed to Bridlington the following Saturday and we were very lucky that day to have fine weather which meant there was only a slight swell on the sea, and when we boarded this wooden Cobble along with another group of about ten people, everyone was optimistic and the general mood was a happy one, that is until we all got out to sea.

At first it was quite exciting, especially on seeing a log the length of two railway sleepers getting sucked down and end up going vertical as it entered the mouth of this big scary whirlpool. It stayed under water at least a minute, which forced the captain to rapidly manoeuvre his boat, and within a few moments of him doing so, this log then shot from out of the sea about thirty yards away and exactly where we had just been. It shot up just like a missile from a Submarine and about four feet into the air, to which the Captain commented that it could have pierced the hull and sunk our boat, but he also chillingly added, that if it had, we wouldn't have been able to swim out of the strength of the whirlpool! On hearing this news I looked at Col and he looked at me and shivers went down both our spines at the same time. Luckily we were soon to be distracted from those feelings of fear and dread when only a little later into the trip we all got to have a big laugh when the few women that were in our company realised that there wasn't any toilets on board, and the little cabin they thought was the toilet was just a store cupboard where the captain kept his fishing gear. Although the laugh was at the women's expense they were also laughing too, because when the males on board had to turn their backs while the women put their bums over the side of the boat for a pee? The blokes kept shouting out daft stuff and cracking jokes to put them off by making them laugh, and the one that did crack everyone up was the comment about a fish that was known to swims up your arse when you went to the toilet at sea! So up until then it was quite an eventful time.

When the laughter had died down however, and there was no distraction from the constant movement of the sea going up and down and up and down I distinctly remember turning green at the time.

But I must have put this experience to the back of my head, because as soon as we reached the area of the wreck where we were to fish I started catching some and the sea sickness suddenly went away, I was too busy pulling up massive Cod every time the four mussel baited hooks hit the bottom, they kept coming up fully loaded with the biggest fish I'd ever seen, and although it was dead tiring to pull them up ,it was a good distraction! There were so many being caught that they were jumping out of everyone's catch baskets and flapping about all over the deck.

The weirdest thing was that for some reason one of Col's uncles couldn't catch one, and no matter what he did the fish wouldn't take his bait, and as each unsuccessful hour passed by the angrier and more frustrated he became. Then towards the end of the day he pulled hard on his fishing rod and it nearly bent double, but the man fishing by his side also got a strike at the same time and when both of their lines came up they were tangled together. Although there was fish on one set of hooks, my mate's uncle insisted they were his, yet the other bloke insisted the same in return. So an argument ensued which got a bit heated between the two, but before it come to blows the Captain swiftly took out his fishing knife and cut the tangle free, letting both the catch and weights drop back into the sea! Unfortunately his action to avoid anymore argument nearly caused another brawl, because just about everyone on board agreed that what the captain did was unnecessary and that the guy who hadn't caught any fish should have had them, and now all the rest of the day trippers were having a go at the Captain for his decision to cut the catch free. The Captain's reply to this was "that it was his boat and he made the rules", and he wasn't apologetic at all. As one can imagine tempers strained between the three man crew and their passengers, and as a consequence before the situation could escalate and turn into a scene from *Mutiny on the Bounty*, the captain had the last word by warning us all of his authority under Admiralty law and as a result we all ended up taking an earlier than usual and silent journey back to shore.

Finally back in the Harbour we loaded our fish that had been already bagged onboard in separate plastic sacks into the car boot to take home, but not before we all gave a share of our catch to my mate's uncle for his empty sack. After we had all weighed him in with a decent haul the five of us went for a slap up dinner and a hot drink of tea in a cafe that was adjacent to the harbour. Just as I had finished licking my plate clean before we set off home, Col's uncles then decided they needed to place a bet at the Bookies on a tip they had got on a horse they had received the night before, and seeing as the race was imminent they were all eager to place the bet and stick around in the Turf accountants for the finish. The trouble was that one of the uncles was overly keen to get across this busy road to place his bet, and the while he was waiting for a gap in the traffic he was stood a bit too far in the road, and when this double decker bus came around the bend, it run over both sets of his is toes! (It was one of those dark blue humped back buses they used to fit perfectly when going through a certain tunnel in Bridlington) This uncle shrieked out really loud and he began hopping from one foot to the other and it looked like he didn't know which foot to rub first. I know we shouldn't have laughed but it was impossible not to, and as a result me and Col got a right telling off, and because the horse lost we experienced yet another quiet journey, but this time home in the car!

So through the mass distraction of the events that took place on that fishing trip I had completely forgot that I did actually get sea sick, and it was only the fact that I had merely overcome the sea sickness in the short term because I was distracted by catching fish, and since that time I had never considered it before, so now was the question could I put up with the constant rolling of the sea day and night for months on end? How would I cope with that I thought? So in answer to the old sea dogs question I didn't tell him the truth, I just nonchalantly replied "we will have to see won't we", only then to see him return me a knowing smile while shaking his head.

On arrival back home in Normanton I couldn't wait to tell my Dad I got the job and that I was leaving home on the following Sunday and I was going to become a Snacker, A TRAINEE FISHERMAN! Of course my Mum knew nothing about any of this, my good news was the first she had heard of it, but as soon as she did she went through the roof mental with my Dad, yelling something like "what the hell have you gone and told him to do this time ya bloody great idiot!" I think were the mildest of her words to start with as I can remember, but later on when my Mum realized I was serious about going, there were a few more colourful ones too. Although it caused a massive rift between the two of them both I was still determined to go, I wasn't going to back out now!

The next few days seemed to pass slowly by, which gave me too much time to think about what I was actually going to do, and in that time I remember whenever I started to get my things together ready to go to Hull, I was only half heartedly packing my little brown leatherette suitcase, because all the while of doing so, all I could think about was that big rusty ship, I just couldn't get that image out of my mind!

So by the time Friday morning came along I was virtually a nervous wreck, I hadn't been sleeping or eating for days and when I woke up that morning I felt sick to the stomach, which wasn't too surprising considering that I was not only assigned to a ship that I thought should have been in a scrap yard, but I also had feelings of trepidation of the rolling seas that was to come as well, not to mention the fact that outside of my youthful pursuits of camping with Army cadets I had never lived away from home before.

That morning I reluctantly climbed out of bed and trudged down stairs full of lacklustre and despair, hoping my Mum's cup of tea would sooth all my worries away. However to my surprise on reaching the bottom step of the staircase I spotted a big brown envelope below the letter box at the foot of the door, and it had NCB printed on it (National Coal Board) that's not all it had my name on it as well? On hurriedly snatching it up from the floor and ripping it open with my teeth like a rabid dog, I was delighted to see it read... Mr Peter McGowan your application for employment has been successful and you are to start work at Sharlston colliery Monday at 6 am to report to the training office on arrival... blah, blah, blah. This was fantastic news, I was ecstatic, it was such a relief to finally get a job at my local colliery, and although it was like jumping out of the fire and back into a frying pan as far as health and safety was concerned, it felt like I had just got off death row in comparison, which made me much happier and I was really looking forward to signing on for work.

Starting Work

Monday couldn't come quickly enough for me and when it did I arrived outside the training office at 6am prompt as stated! Although that being the case to my surprise when I arrived at the training office it was all in darkness, there was no one around at all, so I asked some colliers and other staff that were still bristling about the pit top as to what I was supposed to do and where I was to go, only to be informed that new starters usually came at 8am when the training office was open! Which meant I would have to wait until then, for two hours I waited around like a right proper Narna (as my Mum would say). When 8am came a training officer arrived on the scene, who a short introduction instructed me to go and see the baths attendant to get myself fixed up with a locker and then get changed into my work wear (which in those days was any old clothing you could spare to work in) and report back to him as soon as possible. On my return back to the office though, there was another training officer in attendance, but after introducing myself I didn't get quite the welcome I was expecting, he seemed miffed at me because I hadn't waited for him to take me down to the bath house to get a locker and get fixed up (I found out later after I had been working there a while that it was rumoured this training officer in question delighted in seeing all the young recruits getting naked, so when he missed out on my cute little arse it must have piss him off).

After a few formalities in the training office I was then dispatched to the stockyard where I would stay for three months doing my basic surface training, and afterwards I could expect to be sent for underground training at the area training colliery which was situated at Allerton Bywater, and this colliery just happened to house the headquarters for the North Yorkshire area.

I remember my introduction and the time I spent in the stockyard well. The stockyard foreman was an ex-army ex-underground colliery official who was the type of bloke who was very organised and wanted to always please his superiors by getting every job done. The rest of the crew were a mixed bunch, ranging from old timers from down the pit who were working their last years out in the fresh air, or just ordinary surface men that didn't want to go underground and were just happy working on there. They were a funny bunch, there was an old grumpy one who wore a permanent frown that would put every miserable persons face to shame, and he worked the crane which was used for lifting all the heavy steel equipment and roof supports etc.(This bloke was notorious for his grumpy attitude) There was a jolly one who drove the fork lift and we got on really well together. There was a younger bloke who ran the small diesel train that took supplies to the bank side of the pit shaft who he hardly ever took his hands out of his pockets, hence affording him the nickname of Pockets! We also had an ex-colliery official who by all accounts had a nervous breakdown while working as a deputy underground, and it was rumoured that he was seen with a wooden pole fishing in a hydraulic fluid tank at the coal face, and he was telling his fellow miners to keep quiet or they would scare away all the fish? (A really nice bloke though)

A little later that morning before I had even chance to start any work, I was summoned by a phone call to the stockyard cabin to report to the personnel manager who was called Claude, to which I assumed was an obligatory thing that all new starters had to do. On entering his office I saw this elderly gentleman sat as his desk, my first impression of him was that his face was weathered and he had the similar characteristics to that of President Lyndon Johnson of the USA.

The first thing he said was "Na then lad sit thi-sen darn sithee" and no sooner I did and to my surprise he then went on to lecture me about my attendance, he said that if I was to become a poor time keeper like my brother he wouldn't hesitate to give me the sack, he also went on to tell me he was reluctant to set me on because of his poor attendance record. So after I had explained to him that unlike my brother I was a good time keeper, he then went on to tell me what he expected of me in regards to my future at Sharlston Colliery. However on departing the office and just as I was closing the door behind me, he made a remark that puzzled me at first (That is until I got home) when he said "And tell thi Mum, thus no need to come to see me and ring my neck now".

It turns out that I must have been the only lad in the whole history of the British Coal Mining coal Industry who got his job because his mum had threatened the personnel manager with consequences if he didn't give me one. Apparently my Mum on hearing the news that I was going to be a deep sea fisherman had made a last ditch effort by phoning up the colliery, telling the personnel manager that if her son ever got swept overboard and lost in the icy cold seas of the North Atlantic Ocean, she would hold him responsible and come up to the pit and ring his bloody neck! So if it wasn't for my mum who knows what sort of life I would have led?

Eventually arriving back at the stockyard to report for duty, I was given the task of filling all the 5 tonne pit tubs and flat cars with supplies for underground use, but what a behemoth task it was. I was expected to fill at least forty tubs with timber and heavy concrete blocks, and then strap equipment down on flat cars with load lock chains tight. After that was done each of the tubs and trams contents would then have to marked up with different coloured paint to indicate the prospective districts where they were going underground, i.e. red for the Barnsley seam, blue for development and green for the Birkwood seam, I think yellow for the north east districts? And write the exact gate of the coal face or tunnel heading they were needed with the colour for that seam (Seams of coal got their name from the place where the seam was nearest the surface. Birkwood is actually at the back of my house) If that wasn't enough if I got finished early and before time the foreman would tell me to go help the others who I thought had much easier jobs, so where was the incentive in that I thought?

It wasn't until a month or so went by before I began to suspect that something was amiss about this work arrangement, even though I was prepared for some hard work I thought this was a too much for one person (It is important to mention at this point that when I was a young lad and needed some money I would either have to earn it by either getting someone's coal in or going potato bashing and pea pulling, which meant I was already used to hard work) and my suspicions were only confirmed when a man who was my Dad's old friend who just happened to work repairing the coal tubs at the top of the stockyard came over to speak to me. After a friendly introductory chat he said he felt compelled to tell me that he had been watching me work and he wondered why no one else was giving me a hand. It was then he informed me that I was actually doing the work which was the usual task of about thirty trainees when they all came together to do their surface training in the stockyard, not only that, he also said that there was supposed to be two other men who worked at the pit shaft lower bank side who had hardly anything to do, and they were supposed to help me with the loading! I will always remember his parting words "Steady on lad, they will kill a willing horse". After hearing these revelations I went to see the foreman at the earliest opportunity to ask if this was true, and when I confronted him about the situation he was shocked to hear that I had been doing the job on my own all of that while.

On ferreting out the two blokes who were supposed to give me a hand, my dreams of respite from this heavy burden were almost immediately shattered by the sight of this pair, they were old ex-miners that looked about 70 year old, and no wonder they were hiding out the way I thought, but I also remember feeling slightly guilty at the time for dropping some of this hard graft on these two old blokes. Although I soon learned they were indeed two crafty old buggers who were still very agile and as strong as Sherpa's from the Himalayas.

By the time four month had passed in the Stockyard I was getting a bit worried that I had been forgotten about, and it was only after constant visits to the training office to remind them, my pestering finally paid off and I was allowed to go on my underground training at the area training colliery. This training was essential to prepare a new starter with the working environment underground and to learn all the skills needed to become a coal miner, and because I was under 18 yrs old it meant I would have to do a full 60 days training, whereas if I had being over 18yrs I could have completed it in only 20 days?

Those 60 days of underground training felt like a year though! Not because it was boring, it was just so much of a bind to actually get there. I had to get up at 6 am to catch one bus to Castleford to get the connection to go on to Allerton Bywater, but if one of the buses was running late or too early I might miss the only bus that would get me there in time for going underground, in which case I would either have to have a day off or phone ahead to ask if the instructors would wait for me a while longer before going down the mine, which was very much to the annoyance of the training manager. Although I didn't miss a day's attendance, I think I arrived late on at least 6 occasions, so you can imagine how much it must have pissed the training management off, but it was better to risk his wrath rather than miss a day's attendance, because that meant I still would have to make up the full 60 days. If a trainee had more than a few days absence he would be sent back to his respective pit where there might not be a job available for him because he was set on to become a miner.

I had lots of fun times at Allerton Bywater and some were hilarious! There were approximately around 120 trainees that were all split off into teams of about 10 or 12, and assigned to a particular mining instructor, who would be either an ex-colliery official or someone that was specifically trained for the job, therefore they would have mining science coming out of his ears. Most of the instructors were quite mad ... Honest! One in particular was called Baz and he was built like a pit bull and rather than use kind words of encouragement as a training tool, he chose intimidation instead, none the less he was really funny at the same time, for example: If a trainee had given him some verbal lip he would put him in a cage that was usually used to cover up moving machinery and made to stay there, and if the captive trainee was still lippy to him, Baz would sometimes tease the lad in the cage by eating his snap in front of him, while making comments about how tasty it was and if the lads mum had made it for him he would deliberately provoke the lad by asking how tasty was his mum, and he would always take further delight on finding a chocolate biscuit or cream bun that had been lovingly wrapped for the lads desert and eat that as well. One particular day a trainee disguised his voice over the underground tannoy system to tease Baz, by repeatedly shouting "Baz baby tha- gets- mi", (it was a phrase from TV show at the time) Baz got him alright, because he knew that despite the lad disguising his voice there was only one person who was cheeky enough to dare. Baz got a hold of his thumb and squeezed it until it burst, really! It was also compulsory for everyone in Baz's team to join his weekly lottery card and like it or not they participated.(I remember him taking our group over the last couple of week and I had to join his lottery too! Haha)

There were some right cantankerous training instructors who were old and set in their ways, although there was some that made your day pass with pleasure. There was this one certain instructor who warned us all never to remove our helmets underground, and to reinforce this rule he would swiftly crack the offender over the head with his yard stick, even if the trainee took his helmet off for one second to scratch his head. (A Deputies yard stick was not only a walking aid, but it was also a tool for measuring out the imperial yard long the old way) this instructor hadn't met Sam before! Sam was the sort of lad, who was big and tough and he was brought up rough and he looked and dressed like a Hells Angel, and he maintained a personality that didn't care for authority at all. One day Sam saw this very same instructor remove his helmet (to perhaps wipe the sweat from his brow) and he thought it would be very funny to seize the instructor's yard stick and crack him over the head to teach him his own lesson, which automatically sent everyone into hysterics, because when Sam hit him it not only sounded a bit too hard on his head but it also made the same hollow conk sound that I've heard in every slapstick comedy on TV. This instructor didn't see the funny side of it all; he went incandescent with rage instead. So it was no surprise to us when Sam was put on report and marched out of the pit to see the training manager.

This wasn't his first time either! On our very first day of attendance at the training centre we were all deployed digging trenches on the pit top and in full view of the training centre offices, which was probably carried by the instructors so they could observe how we all worked together, and who were competent and who were the complete idiots, and they didn't have to wait long to find that out. This was when Sam decided he'd had enough of wheel barrowing and thought it clever to stick a pick blade straight through the wheel barrow tyre to render it useless.

There was yet another Sam incident in the underground training galleries (These were a part of the working mine that were sectioned off and made safe for training purposes only) when one of the trainees thought it was amusing to put some-one else's water bottle on a roof support tie bar, and then he invited everyone to throw lumps of rock at it to see who would be the first to knock it off. As soon as Sam saw what we were all doing he couldn't wait to join in the mischief, he was more than eager to have a go, and pushing everyone to one side with this huge lump of rock in his hand he hit this clear plastic bottle dead centre and totally demolished it on his first throw, which burst wide open and making its contents splash everywhere. Even before this now useless bottle had hit the deck Sam was already jubilantly jumping up and down excitedly and exclaiming that he was the champion! While everyone else was in hysterics laughing and pointing at Sam celebrating his throwing skills, who just joined in the fun and began laughing as well. That is until he realised whose bottle it was he had just splattered, because it turned out it was his!

He went mental when he realised it was his own bottle and to everyone's horror he then suddenly pulled out a flick knife from his pocket and he began lunging at anyone that was still laughing at him. In fear of being stabbed everyone just set off running towards the pit bottom as fast as they could, we weren't stopping for no one, especially with this angry long haired frothing at mouth loon that looked like something from a slash horror movie chasing us with a flick knife, we just kept running for our lives and for the safety of the pit bottom, where we was sure most of the other instructors and everyone else would be waiting to ride out the mine and we would be safe. Unbeknownst to us though, just around the next bend to the pit bottom some miner's had only just finished resurfacing a section of concrete floor and when about twenty of us came bounding around the corner in panic, we couldn't avoid running through this 20 yards of freshly laid concrete that had only just been tamped to perfection. We all got a severe warning for that and we all assumed that this time Sam would definitely get the sack and it would be the last we would see of him, but to everyone's astonishment he didn't get the sack and we did see him again?

The next time I saw him was on the first day of technical college where we had to attend one day a week on a Monday to study mining science, which was a part of the mining craft program introduced in 1975 that allowed an ordinary miner the opportunity to sign up as a student for a four year period, and if they completed the full course and passed all the exams, they could then either become a Deputy or an Over man. If the student went further towards higher education he could achieve a HNC in mining, which included electrical and mechanical engineers certificates, they would then have all the qualifications required to become a colliery manager. I decided to sign up for the full course because I knew I had a bit of a brain and I realised that I might want a change from just being an ordinary miner in years to come, besides that it was a day out of the pit!

This particular day on entering the college canteen area, the only person I could see that knew me was Sam, so it was natural we would sit together, but on taking my seat I noticed that just about everyone else in the canteen was staring at Sam, who was not only wearing this biker jacket that had his biker club rockers colours displayed across his back, but also a neckerchief headband over his head, which must have looked quite intimidating to some of these young lads. If that wasn't bad enough Sam then pulled out this old style miners underground snap tin from his leather jacket, from which he then produced the biggest doorstep jam sandwiches I'd have ever seen in my life, they must have been at least three inch thick and the funny thing was when Sam began biting into one, the mass of jam that was inside squirted out and ran down his chin, and for anyone who was already watching this amusing spectacle it was virtually impossible for them to hold back the laughter. Although most were covering their mouths trying to hide their sniggers from this big scary man, they were still pretty obvious to Sam, who reacted in the only way he knew how by jumping to his feet and going into a rage and marching around each of the tables where the sniggers were coming from and shouting in their faces, spit an all "what you looking at, what's so funny" and frightening them half to death in the process. They had never seen anything like him before, and all who had received Sam's wrath were very noticeable by the way they were left cowering lower in their seats!

Apparently there was even another incident in the gym but I wasn't present at the time and for reasons I will explain about later in my story, but it went something like this: There was this PT instructor at the college gym and he was a little fat man who had the small man complex, and his character was very close to that of the PE instructor in the film *Kez*. His party piece was besides smacking a trainee around the ear hole for being cheeky towards him, was that he would often make example of a bigger lad who might not have been listening or may have been misbehaving, and him being an ex-boxing champion he would challenge them in the ring hoping to teach them a lesson they would never forget. That is until he met Sam! I never got to hear the full details of that incident, but I can imagine!

Eventually I completed the full 60 days underground training in the galleries and I could now set a wooden roof prop, a hydraulic prop, advance and set a hydraulic chock, splice a rope, zip a conveyor belt, put stone dust barriers up, lay rail track and was competent in a plethora of other mining skills and as a bonus I got to run through a course of freshly laid concrete, which was something I've always wanted to do, and now I was ready to become a real miner!

What made my completion of training at Allerton Bywater even the more special was when I went to collect my last pay packet there? On receiving it I noticed it was extraordinarily fatter than usual, on opening it I found out why, it had got my tax return inside! (This was because I had been put on a temporary emergency tax code and when I received my final wages at Allerton Bywater I also got a proper tax code, which meant I got a tax return from the Inland Revenue, which put another £60 on top of my wage that was usually about £12 for the week) It was like winning the football pools to me! Although it wasn't the size of the likes of Viv Nicolson's fortune, it was the most money I had ever had in my life and I was determined I wasn't going to fritter it away like she did.

Nonetheless in the coming days a strange temptation was put there?

It happened one day when I bumped into one of my fellow trainee miner buddies that just happened to live in my home town and in an adjacent street, who like me had also received a sizeable tax return, but his mind was already made up and he was dead set on buying a big tropical fish tank with his extra bonus, and he tried to convince me to do the same?

I've got to admit that when I accompanied him to the Aquarium centre and saw for the first time how magically all the fish looked when were lit up by the ultraviolet light in their tanks, I nearly went for it and bought one, especially when I saw all the different types of coloured fish, each with their own particular features and plants, all made up to look like miniature scenes from beneath the Sea. To me they resembled little worlds which I imagined one could easily get lost in, and particularly on those days when our world wasn't looking so good to us, and where one could also unwind by spending the time to add little details, like little ship wrecks or a treasure chest that made bubbles when the lid popped up, just to help the mind escape the rigors of life perhaps?

My mate ended up buying practically the biggest tank in the shop and all the fish and all the paraphernalia that went with it. He had explained to me beforehand of how each particular fish had its own job in the tank that would service each of the other fish's requirements by keeping the tank clean thus enabling them to socially live together, which all sounded really interesting. After we eventually got his tank home he went to straight to work setting it all up in his bedroom and first thing he had to do was test it for leaks, and although it didn't, he still had to wait a week for all the tap water to purify before he could stock it with fish. No sooner had the water in his tank tested safe he went for his fish, and after stocking his Aquarium he invited me round. When he shut the curtains and switched on the tanks ultraviolet light for the first time the tank lit up all the fish inside did too, and with all the added background and plants and scenery it looked amazing, we were both mesmerised, we sat and watched the fish in the tank for hours. After a while of this fish tank staring though my natural common sense kicked in and it was telling me that the novelty of it would wear off in no time at all, and my much needed earnings could be better spent than on a tropical fish tank! And I was right about the novelty of it all, because within a year of my mate buying his Aquarium his lack of interest became obviously noticeable by the colour of the water in his fish tank which got greener each successive time I visited him, and it wasn't long afterwards he sold it for a fraction of the price.

A Fully Trained Miner

Having now been fully underground trained as a miner I was ready for action, and soon found myself back at my own colliery where one would think things would start to progress and get better, but they didn't things were about to get worse.

That first Monday morning I had arrived at the training office at 8am prompt this time and already present there was another lad who was also fresh from his underground training at the centre, but he was 18 and he would have only had to do 20 days training with the seniors groups which meant our paths wouldn't have crossed much. This other new starter though, who I can only describe as not being the sharpest tool in the box was given better consideration over me because his dad had already asked if he could be allowed to work with his son so he could keep a close eye on him, and seeing as the only two available places where they were short handed underground were either the pit bottom or in-bye on supplies where the better money could be earned, and because his dad was already working in-bye on supplies in the exact place in-bye where they were short handed, you can guess where I was sent?

The Pit Bottom

The pit bottom was one of the worst places to work in the whole mine, firstly because it was the lowest paid job and secondly because it meant I would be on the job straight away and down the pit before everyone else. To make my first day introduction worse I had to wear a brand new shiny bright yellow helmet and a bright yellow cap lamp rim to show everyone that I was a cherry and still a trainee, which also meant I had to have 20 days close personal supervision of a senior all the while I was underground. They might as well pinned a big badge on me that said virgin on it at the same time. I know that attitude sounds odd but I guess at that age I was in too much of a hurry to become a man and prove my worth? And just when I thought things couldn't get any worse they did, and this was when I went to descend the shaft to get to this particular pit bottom. The first thing that struck me on landing in the shaft bottom was that it was absolutely freezing cold and I was only wearing light gear ready do hot sweaty graft, because I never thought in a million years I would have ended up working there.

I couldn't believe it, even though I had previously checked by asking this bloke in the lockers if the pit bottom was warm or cold, and he said it was warm, but the thing is there were two pit bottoms, one was an up cast shaft which expels all the warm exhaust air from the whole mine and the other was a downcast shaft that fetches in all the freezing fresh cold air down the pit to ventilate it. So there I was to work in what I can only describe as a freezing wind tunnel, and now facing a terrible situation all because I wasn't specific enough in my original enquiry to receive the right information.

(Which immediately reminded me of an old joke that goes something like this: A man walks into a pub where a man is already stood at the bar with a massive dog besides his leg, so being cautious the new customer on approaching the bar asked him if his dog bites, to which the man at the bar replied "no", so the other man proceeds to pet this massive dog which instantly savages the poor bloke's arm, who then begins to shout his protest, "I thought your dog didn't bite" Only to hear the man at the bar then reply, "It's not my dog"!)

The first bloke I came across on descending the pit shaft was the Onsetter who lifted the safety gate to unload the men off the cage in the pit bottom when men were riding the shaft, he also loaded the 5 tonne tubs of coal to go up to the surface. My first impression of him was that he looked like that convict ringleader in the film *The Prison Break*, starring Laurel and Hardy. He looked me up down like a new fresh piece of meat and spitting tobacco juice at my feet he said "Are you McGowan or something", and after acknowledging that I was he then told me I was to report to the deputies cabin further up the road way, but when he said this I noticed he said it with air of contempt. (Later that day I was soon to find out that he certainly lived up to the image of the character I had already given him).

I walked up this long tunnel road way towards where I was told to go and where there was lots of lights and activity. On arrival I could see that a cabin had been cut out of the rock and then built in with brick, and like everything else it was painted white. Above the door a sign read Pit Bottom Office, and just as I was about to enter this tunnel like entrance I was met in the doorway by the pit bottom deputy who was just walking out, but I didn't quite get the reception I was expecting, no sooner I introduced myself he began questioning me as to where I had been up until now, stating that I should have been there at 6am not 9am, so after taking a deep breath I explained it was my first day back from the area training colliery, and that I had to report to the training officer to get sorted out there first before being deployed to where I was going. On hearing my explanation he became much happier and less grumpy and we started to get on fine after that.

Then appearing by his side was this other old miner that looked to be nearing retirement age, who introduced himself as Dunk! He had a kind and softly spoken voice when he went on to tell me that he was my going to be my close personal supervisor and I was to be with him for the next 20 days period, in which time he was going to show me the ropes of how everything there worked. But before we could get started Dunk noticed that I was shivering uncontrollably and nearly blue with the cold, so he insisted that I had to go straight out of the pit to get a docket from the personnel manager, so I could then receive a donkey jacket coat from the stores.

Which I thought was great at first, but then I remembered my last conversation with the personnel manager and I didn't want to become a nuisance on my first day underground, so I was a bit reluctant to go, but when I told Dunk the reason why he just laughed and encouraged me on by assuring me it would be ok. No sooner I stepped from the cage and on the surface I went straight over to the personnel manager's office as ordered. On arrival there I was still a bit reluctant to bother Claude, so I only knocked on his door gently half hoping he wasn't in, even so the door wasn't closed properly and it opened for me as I knocked. On peering around the door I saw that he was indeed in, and the first thing he said on seeing my face was "it's thee again is it, what duz thy want nar" Fortunately he said it in a sarcastic and half jokingly way, which made me much happier about making my request, to which I then very humbly asked for a pit issue donkey jacket, by telling him in a very pitiful voice of how I was unexpectedly sent to work in the freezing pit bottom, also stating that all the other pit bottom staff said I should automatically qualify for one working there! Only to hear him reply "Thaz no chance, fetch a coyt from home, nar get this sen lost and shut door behind thi". So that was that as far as a donkey jacket was concerned I thought, but just as I was about to close the door behind me, and without any forethought I couldn't help make the sarcastic reply in return, "What's difference does it make between me freezing to death in the North Atlantic seas or here in the pit bottom, my Mum will still come to see you and ring your neck!" Which Claude thought was quite amusing and made him laugh all the while he was writing out a docket for my new Donkey jacket coat. Although on leaving the office it wasn't without hearing him shout, "dun't let mi see thee in here again... for a very long time, sithee"!

I was soon back in the pit bottom to restart my induction training and because there was probably only a couple of hours left in the shift, Dunk whisked me around all the workings just to get me acquainted with the pit bottom surroundings. Afterwards we found ourselves spending the remaining time sat in the Onsetter's cabin until it was time to ride out of the mine, where there was an electric heater and it was warm.

The only fringe benefit of working in the pit bottom was that we got out of the pit on the first ride up the shaft before the rest of the men arrived in the pit bottom from in-bye, which was a bonus because there was a half hour difference between the first riders and the last man out, and it also meant we could get a good choice of shower because it was often the case that some of the showers were either too hot or too cold, and on some occasions the water would only trickle out. It was essential to land on a good one so I could get showered in comfort and not have to rush to make the 181 bus home. If I missed this one the next wasn't until an hour later!

However in the short time we spent in this Onsetters cabin waiting for the winder to signal down to the pit bottom that it was the men's riding time, this Convict 99 character kept staring at me, not only that he was purposely spitting his tobacco juice onto my boots and my toecaps were now covered in this brown stinking tobacco spit. To tell you the truth it shocked me, I didn't know how to react to this at first, so I just gave him the "are you fucking serious you're having a laugh aren't you" sort of look, to which he just replied by spitting on my boot again, followed a grinning smirk.

Little did Convict 99 know that despite my young and innocent appearance in my shiny new yellow virgin helmet, he was trying to intimidate someone who had been around a bit, an ex-football hooligan who had been in and out of courts from being a juvenile and wasn't unaccustomed to a bit of violence and intimidation. That being said I didn't react in the manner I normally would have, because although he was acting tough he was still an old man and I was brought up to respect the older generations and I didn't particularly fancy falling out with anyone, especially on my first day on the job, I was just so grateful to actually be in employment, so rather than do something really stupid and lose my job, and then have to hear my Dad's words in my head "what have you done this time" I just spat on his boots and stared back at him instead, to which he just grinned and turned his head and did a Muttley the dog type of snigger.

I think he was testing my metal? After that day he wasn't too bad and we got on ok. Although I did see him have fight one day in the pit bottom with another notorious tough guy called the Demon! They went at each other with coupling hooks (A bar with a handle about 3ft long with hook that was used to couple trains) they were clashing them together just like it was a sword fight, going at each other hammer and tong, resulting in them both receiving some nasty cuts and bruises about their heads. But this sort of thing was normal in those days! For instance, if someone in temper called a man a bastard it was more likely that he would be punched in the face and everyone would say he deserved it.

When my first shift in the pit bottom was over I couldn't wait to get showered and go home, I certainly wasn't relishing the thought of going back to work in that place again, but I needed the job and the money, and there was no way I was going to let myself and my family down, so it was a case of just grinning and bearing it for the time being, besides I had one day a week of respite from the pit while attending the training college at Whitwood, and I could still dream of the day when I became a colliery manager!

Which reminds me of another story...

Although I wasn't officially attending school at the time, my mate Swag had convinced me to go with him on an underground visit to a local colliery by way of a careers program from school. The invitation happened after I received a letter at my home requesting me to attend the careers office at school, and it was coming out of this interview which I can only describe as not being a very happy one, it was more like receiving a telling off than a employment discussion, in fact it very much like the careers scene from the film *Kes*, and that's when I bumped into my mate Swag who was sat outside the office awaiting his interview and he informed me of an organised trip from school to the local colliery at Ackworth, but he also told me that for some reason we had to be in school uniform to go? Although I didn't fancy adorning that uniform ever again, I did fancy a trip down a pit!

When the trip day came me and Swag stood waiting in place to board a coach which was already waiting at the school gates, when this teacher turned up with a clipboard in his hand, and the first thing he said was "where is everyone else" because there was only me and Swag there in attendance. Although we both explained that our names were the only ones added to the list that was put up on the wall, and that no one else was interested in going, this teacher wouldn't hear any of it, he was insistent there was still others to come even though we had to be at the colliery at a certain time, he totally ignored the schedule and held the bus up half an hour to wait around just in case, regardless of me and Swag showing him the original list of people volunteering to go!

Eventually we arrived Ackton Hall Colliery where we met by some men in suits who seemed a bit upset and put out that we weren't on time, who then quickly herded us into this office, only to present us then in front of this angry looking man, who immediately went into a red faced tirade about our late arrival. This personal manager was so angry he must have intimidated our teacher so much that he decided to put the blame for our lateness on me and Swag to get himself off the hook?

The reason why this personnel manager was so annoyed was because we had missed the riding times for the transport underground, which he explained was called the Man Rider, and it would take another hour to get back to the pit bottom from the journey in-bye that we should have been on, if we had arrived on time. (The man rider was like the carriages on the big dipper in an amusement park, but you could sit four or five abreast, and it was pulled by steel rope.) So we now had an hour to kill sat in an office with this un amused personnel manager looking at us as though he hated us, who kept mumbling to himself but loud enough so we all could hear, about how late home he was going to be.

When he eventually calmed down and he became a bit more human he gave us a drink of pop in a bottle that was from the local Heys Brothers pop factory in Featherstone, which he must have kept especially for when visitors came. The personnel manager then began filling the rest of the time in by telling us about mining, and then he got on to talking about methane gas situations underground, all the while he was offering the two of us participation by asking questions to gauge our knowledge of understanding. One particular question arose when he stated that if the mine got a 2.5% gas reading all the men would have to be evacuated, and one of his questions was what is the conversion of 2.5 % to fraction, but neither of us could tell him the answer, I did know but when someone is browbeating me I can't think, and because we both remained silent he became full of scorn at our ignorance and lack of education. All the while he was lecturing the two of us about how thick we both were, this teacher was shaking his head at us both and also wearing the same look of disgust on his face too, that is until the personnel manager dropped the ball into his lap for him to give everyone the answer, in fact he said "go on, tell them" assured the teacher could, only to see the teacher's face turn bright red and then he began stuttering, obviously stalling for time and the best he could come out with was, "you can't expect me to know that I'm a Geography teacher!"

At hearing this excuse the personnel manager went nuts again and into another tirade, he gave this teacher a right old dressing down. The funny thing was that when we first introduced ourselves to this personnel manager I had told him I wanted to be a Electrician or a Fitter in the coal industry like my brother, and he was very supportive, but now he was pouring scorn on us saying "that if either of us ever came to him for a job he wouldn't even give us one sweeping the car park!"

That hour in that office was the longest hour in the world, and the rest of the day didn't get any better either. When we went to get changed in the pit baths we were only given some colliery issue overalls and knee pads and boots, and on seeing both me and Swag putting them on this personnel manager was shocked that we hadn't fetched our old clothes to go underneath, and because of this we had to wear part of our school uniforms instead. Little did we know at the time that we were going down a up-cast shaft where the air was exhausting from the mine and it was really warm, and when we eventually descended the shaft and arrived in its pit bottom, it was noticeable that all the men were working in shorts and vests only, and there was me and Swag with overalls on with part our school uniforms on underneath.

We then boarded an awaiting Man rider and no sooner we did the attendant rang the signal bell, two rings then another two and the Man-rider set off, slowly at first then accelerating into a break neck speed down into what looked like a big hole in the floor, which turned out to be a steep drift that went hundreds of metres deeper than the shaft bottom we had just arrived from, it seemed to be going downwardly for ages before it stopped at its final destination. After we had arrived at that particular coal seam level we alighted the transport where we were then told we still had a bit of a march to go, which turned out to be a trek of about 30 minutes or so. All the while tramping this personnel manager was doing his job by pointing out things of interest by the use of his cap lamp beam, and again he kept asking us all questions along the way. One question after another he asked and every time he directed one at Swag, three times in succession he answered him by saying "What", but on the third time of this manager hearing that same reply he went nuts again, he told Swag that if he said what one more time, he would give his ear a clout! (Swags ears hadn't adjusted to the underground pressure yet and they needed to pop, just like when you are on an aeroplane, so it wasn't his fault he was partially deaf)

Eventually we arrived at the coal face and by this time we knew we were near where all the action was because the noise of the machinery got louder and the airborne dust was now very heavy in our cap lamp beams. There was lots of activity at the coal face and I remember we were told to wait a few moments until the situation was safe, and only then were we allowed to duck into this very noisy small opening that was the coal face, where we then had to start crawling on our hands and knees down this long dusty tunnel of roof supports towards these hazy distant cap lamp beams and the noises of the coal cutting that was actually taking place.

As we crawled further the dust got thicker and noise got louder and those distant beams of lights we saw, were now shining directly in our faces, coming from inquisitive coal face workers who each in turn had their little joke and performed their party piece they had saved for when visitors came. What made things worse besides all the dust and din was the fact the face men were ramming the coal panzer chain forward towards the coal face to catch the coal, and we were now having to crawl over all these rams as they extended outwardly, which was very unnerving and I distinctly remember being a bit worried that I might get my hands or knees trapped in the ram couplings, and all the while I was nervously crawling over these moving rams and couplings, I couldn't help notice the look of delight on the miners faces to see the panic on mine. It was a long crawl and by the time we reached the other end both me and Swag were exhausted and dripping wet through with sweat and although that ordeal was over, we still had to tramp back to the Man-rider to make our way out the mine, but as we did we didn't realise how much trouble our late arrival would cause in the end.

When the four of us eventually entered the pit bottom area to go up the shaft and out of the pit, the personnel manager saw a handful of men walking to the pit bottom and where they wasn't supposed to be, who were very surprised to see this personnel manager underground at that time of the day, and by all accounts from what we could make out from the following loud conversation he had caught these guys trying to sneak out of the pit early, and he was giving them a right bollocking, he took all their check numbers and put them all on report!

So it wasn't the most positive day I've ever had but looking back it was a really funny experience, and here's the thing, all my life is full of experiences like this.....Honest!

The next shift at Sharlston came too fast for me, I had to be up at 4.45am to get to the pit and be ready to go down the mine before 5.45am. On arrival at the colliery I stepped off the pit bus that was laid on by the coal board for the miners that came from Normanton and the Castleford area (the Paddy bus) and headed straight to a packed canteen which was already brisling with activity to join the queue to get the obligatory cup of tea and a bacon sarny, just like everyone else did. And this is when the daily queuing process began, which continued right throughout every stage of getting ready to start a shift. Firstly having to queue in a packed canteen, then everyone moving on together to the next queue to receive their underground checks from the time office (these were two metal discs that had the miners' personal works number on, one brass and one silver, that when handed in to the Banksman at the shaft side, silver for going down and brass on returning, did exactly what the name suggest, because they were issued to check who was in or out of the mine. Other pits called them tallies). Next busy place was the lockers where we had to get undressed at our clean locker then walk around naked to our dirty locker to put our work gear on, and to prevent crowding of space they provided top and bottom lockers, which meant that most of the time men eager to get dressed virtually had to climb over each other to get their gear on, and if getting someone's arse or bollocks in your face half the time wasn't bad enough, there was some right grumpy old twats who would take advantage of your youthful naivety by insisting you waited for them to get out the way first. The next stage was at the lamp room where miners would get their own personal lamp and a self rescuing pod that matched their own check number (a self rescuer was a device to put on your belt which became your breathing apparatus if a fire broke out underground and it was supposed to help you breath in conditions with carbon monoxide present in the air) after the lamp room everyone would have to queue to board the pit cage at the Bankside. And virtually all to be done again but in reverse order on the return journey! So I reckon we spent a biggest part of our day queuing?

The Lamp room was the last gathering place on the surface before going underground and this immediate area was soon bristling with a full mixture of men, some were huge and stocky and some like me were tall and slim, and there was some very small ones who I imagined that if they had been conscripted into the Vietnam War, they would have ended up as tunnel rats whose job it was to go down the Victor Charlie bunker holes to root them out?

Everyone would be wearing their old clothes they had fetched from home and noticeable by the way each one dressed, it gave a good indication of what their jobs were underground. Rippers usually wore their old worn out rugby shirts either from their amateur or professional careers, and they usually wore waistcoats too, but the biggest give away was the size of the water containers they carried which indicated the dryness of their job. Some older colliers wore what looked like their old suits, some even still wore wooden clogs, and the smaller men in boiler suits (Tunnel Rats) usually worked on the coal face waste system, others usually had some form of tool or specialist thing that identified their skill or trade underground. You could also recognise the generation of each miner by what style of helmet they wore (modern ones were heavy plastic and were a bit bulky and sat higher on the head, the oldest ones were low on the head and they were made of a thin shell like material and some later ones were made of hard folded over leather material that was riveted together).

There were about 300 men on a typical day shift of all ages every shape and size. There were Face men, Tunneller's, Supply men, Belt men, Craft's men, and there were also underground officials of the management staff, who were easily recognisable by the shiny Davy lamps that hung from their belts, and depending on their status some would also carry a yard stick as well.

A lot of the men would also be carrying equipment, some would be carrying explosives, cutter picks, hydraulic hoses and all manner of heavy objects that were urgently needed underground, so these men always got to the front of the queue to board the cage.

I distinctly remember standing outside the lamp room just after getting my pit lamp and self rescuer and just having my last cigarette before heading to the Bankside to go down the mine, when my mates from Normanton who had already been at Sharlston about six month beforehand, spotted me standing there on my own and came over for a chat. They were all eager to find out where I was working and when I told them everyone laughed, but it was mostly a pity type of laugh than anything else, except from one of my mates who thought it was hilarious that I was actually sent to a place of work doing what he considered was an old man's job, and he kept making jokes about it all the while. We all eventually joined the long queue to go underground, and although I was a pit bottom man and was supposed to go underground before everyone else, that morning we rode the cage together. Once in the pit bottom we then headed to where the diesels were parked ready and awaiting to pull two long trains of empty 5 tonne coal tubs that took the workforce in-bye and to the workings.

I've got to admit that when me and my mates parted company, knowing they were going to where all the real work was and money could be earned I was quite envious but I tried not to show it, all I could do was stand there and watch on like someone who had bought a platform ticket only.

The Shunter then blew his whistle and waved his cap lamp at the driver signalling for him to set off, and just before it did I heard a loud voice calling out my name, and it was coming from the pit bottom deputy who was deploying a small crowd of men that were outside the cabin office, and he was looking for me, and because I didn't answer straight away, he shouted it out the second time "PETE MCGOWAN, PIT BOTTOM" which sounded so definite, and it didn't make me feel too happy being reminded about it in the first place, but to make things worse, no sooner had the deputy shouted my name out it was immediately followed a spontaneous cry of laughter and it was coming from the same tub all my mates were sat in, to which at first I wanted to believe that they were just having a laugh between themselves, but trusting my instincts and knowing my mates better, I knew deep down they were laughing at me and it was more than likely at my sad predicament being stuck there working in the cold and freezing my bollocks off all shift long, and my suspicion was solidly confirmed when I heard one of my mates, the very same one who had been taking the piss from the start, shout out, but in a sarcastic way, "PETE MCGOWAN BOT PITTOM" purposely reversing its name to give it more of a comedy effect, and somehow making it sound a sadder place than it was, and funnily enough we only ever referred to it as the Bot-Pittom from that day on!

The two trains finally pulled away each in turn heading up this long tunnel towards in-by that looked to stretch for miles on end, so I stood for a while to watch the rear red light of the train as it grew smaller in the distance, and believe it or not in those last moments as the Manrider train's rear light was just going out of focus, I was almost sure I heard another faint cry of "Pete McGowan Bot-Pittom" being shouted by my mates.

In those very final moments of their departure though, when all the noises of men had finally gone, the Bot-Pittom suddenly became relatively quiet in comparison and I distinctly remember at that very moment getting a familiar feeling of loneliness, which was a reoccurring feeling I had experienced in the past. I think it stems from when we were young kids, when after my Mum and Dad would have a fall out, which would often result in my Mum and us kids having to part company from my Dad a few times or vice versa, and this sometimes meant we would have short stays at my Granny and Granddad's house, which at my age seemed to be miles away, although it was only on the edge of town. In actual fact they lived in the same school yard where I attended school, and because me and my brother had to get there by bus, it made it feel like it was far away. Granddad and Grandma only lived there because they used to be the school caretakers at that school at one point, and after retirement they stayed in the house because they actually owned it.

Sometimes we would have to spend a couple of weeks there at a time and every day when all the other kids went home, I was left to a silent empty playground with no one else to play with, so I think this linked together with separation of my parents

Diesel locomotive. ©NCMME

5 tonne tubs. ©NCMME/HaroldWhite Collection

somehow imprinted the fear of abandonment into my psychology, and if any form of this would occur I used to be overcome with a deep sense of loneliness. It was worse at my Grannies' on the weekends because there weren't any younger kids living around that area, everyone in this particular isolated row of houses were old fogeys to me. I still had a older brother and sister for a bit of company so I guess it wasn't all that bad, none the less that feeling of loneliness used to repeat itself even in the slightest of circumstances, and that's exactly how I felt that day in the Bot-Pittom.

In the 20 days constant close supervision with Dunk I soon found out he was a nice and mild mannered sort of bloke, I never saw him lose his cool once, not that I gave him any cause to, he was just a nice guy! He also had a face that I imagined wouldn't have required much face paint to make a good circus clown because he already had the natural smiley facial lines and features a clown had? His job was to train me on every job there and when I was fully trained I could then be signed to any particular job in the Bot-Pittom.

While Dunk was acting as my instructor we often found ourselves with some spare time on our hands and on those occasions we would either go exploring or sometimes we would also accompany the pit bottom deputy on his safety checks around the underground areas he was responsible for. (This was a large area that encompassed the whole Bot-Pittom and all the old workings that still had to be ventilated. His safety checks consisted of a series of tests, one for methane gas by use of his Davey lamp, he also had a electronic device that tested for carbon dioxide and a manual pump with a crystal tube that was called a Draiger that detected carbon monoxide, and if that was present it could only mean one thing, there was a fire somewhere? He also had to make sure the roof was secure and the walkways were clear and everything was safe).

A part of his inspection route took us through the old underground stables where the pit ponies were once kept not too many years beforehand, it was all very interesting and more like visiting a museum for the day than being at work. Harnesses and horse gear still hung from hooks where they must have been placed the very last time they were used. Although the ponies were long gone, some horse hair and straw still remained and you could still smell their aroma in the air, but there was also another overpowering smell, and the culprits for this was the unfortunate legacy of fetching straw underground to feed the ponies, and that was... Mice!

From there we journeyed down to the bottom of the Haigh Moor shaft sump, which was the very bottom of our up cast shaft at Sharlston, and where I met two men who were permanently deployed there to shovel away all the spillage that fell down the shaft from the skips that were being filled with coal at different levels higher up to be hoisted out of the mine.

One time we rode down an underground shaft that just took us to a lower level, then we rode back up the main shaft to the Haigh Moor seam which had been worked out long ago, but this level was always kept manned all the three shifts for the loading of coal that came from the rest of the mine, which eventually went into the skips that took it up the shaft and to the surface. I remember this occasion well because in all my years at Sharlston Colliery it was the only time I actually bumped into my uncle Ted who was the deputy in charge of that area.

My uncle Ted was a real strange one though; it struck me at the time on meeting him that day that he could hardly bring himself to acknowledge me at all, even though I was his nephew! To be honest it didn't totally surprise me, because in the good old days when relatives used visit our house they would be all formerly dressed in their best suits and the women would wear what I would describe at today's standards as wedding clothes, on these types of get-togethers uncle Ted would seem to stay pretty quiet regardless of how much merriment there was, he always managed to remain slightly austere throughout. I was later told that prior to Uncle Ted's WW2 experience of suffering at the hands of the

Japanese as a prisoner of war; he was a very jolly chap, so I always took that into consideration. There was only a hand full of men who worked up there and they were all of a similar age as Uncle Ted and nearing retirement, and because all these job areas were isolated it probably suited his and the others' requirements being on their own, plus they were steady jobs with no hard graft or hassle involved, all they had to do was sit at a transfer point or a underground bunker systems and watch the coal travel from in-bye to the shaft side.

Each man could be hundreds of meters from the next and sometimes they wouldn't see another person until the end of the shift. The weird thing was that there was an accumulation of foreigners working in that area, who were either Czechs, Polish, Ukrainian, Yugoslavian and others who didn't seem to want to talk much, and it was rumoured that one or two of them had fled their own country in WW2, some fleeing from Nazis invading their country, but it was also rumoured that some fled after the war because they had been fighting or collaborating with the Nazis? There was a bit of a joke that the butcher of Prague was working up there, and all the while the famous Nazi hunter Simon Wiesenthal was running around in exotic places on the South American continent looking for Nazis, the reason he was unable to find the main ones was because they were all actually working at Sharlston Colliery loading coal in the Haig Moor pit bottom?

The one thing in common about all the Pit bottoms was that no matter which colliery they were located they were normally the oldest parts of the mine, this is because these were the areas underground that obviously had to be mined firsthand, therefore from those early beginnings and there on afterwards the pit bottom would have served as the main artery of all the activity that ebbed and flowed throughout the whole lifespan of that particular part of the mine. And in all those decades and sometimes hundred years or more, there would be no doubt that these areas would have experienced every conceivable human emotion possible in those periods of time, and taking into consideration that it is scientifically proven that energy cannot be destroyed but can only diminish, it would be fair to say that the residue of all those emotions and experiences, which in some cases could be really grim, could be permanently embedded into the atmosphere in those particular locations? And on the odd occasion all the energy of all those emotions and memories might sometimes permeate from out of the rock and into the ether, and somehow like a recording of an event, which at certain times might be re-enacted and repeated every now and then?

In the early days pit bottoms were dangerous places because everything had to be done by hand it was also very hard work, which meant a lot of blood sweat and tears and a few accidents over the years. There will have been times of anger, fear and panic and all causes of despair, and sometimes feelings of sadness and grief when a workmate was killed down there!

So it was no wonder then that Pit bottoms were notoriously known for been the spookiest areas underground, well spooky to some that is, for those who had a natural nervous dispositions, whereas most of the miners I came across were all tough and thick skinned, they would normally laugh at such notions and dismiss them as nonsense, or typically make the comment "it was all a load of bollocks!"

And then there were folks like me who shared a certain nature that is common to us of the fair skinned and reddish/ginger haired community, which is having a very sensitive nervous systems that not only makes you sensitive on the inside, but also on the outside too, thus heightening the senses of awareness.

On occasions I would sense things others might not, for instance, I would feel it if the atmosphere changed and sometimes I would get a detached feeling if something wasn't quite right, on the odd occasion I would experience feelings of déjà vu. Other types of people can have heightened senses too, but it's more common in us ginners and Celtic types. I don't in any way claim to be a super sensitive like a psychic or medium, but I'm definitely higher up that scale than most normal folk, and on top of that I have a very inquisitive personality by nature and like to get to the bottom of things as well, so I guess I look into things others wouldn't bother with, and you know what they say, if you don't look you won't see?

All around the Bot-Pittom where I worked I often got the feeling that someone was watching me, which was solidly confirmed one day when our regular deputy fell ill, and in his place the seam Over man sent us a man called Harold, who just happened to be the top Spiritualist in the whole of the North of England! From that day on he told me just about every ghost story he knew, day after day I would hear one story after another of all the houses and places he had been asked to cleanse of ghosts or spirits as he preferred to call them.

He really freaked me out one day when we were both sat in the old tool cabin where the machine cutter picks were usually stored, and he then told me and actually pointed with his finger as he did, that there was a spirit sat beside me on the wooden bench I was sat on, and that this spirit was listening to our conversation. I can distinctly remember getting the feeling that something was odd a while before he told me this, and when he went on to explain that it was a spirit of a young boy miner who comes to visit now and then, I believed him straight away! A young lad I knew had refused to work in a certain place because he kept seeing the ghost of the same young boy. It was rumoured there was small bare foot prints in the stone dust on the ground in the location where the sighting had occurred, and it was also said that the young man who had seen it went into a state of shock and he had to be sent home from the mine. These types of incidents weren't that regular, but I recall these sorts of things happening several times over the years that I worked at Sharlston.

On one of these occasions a young man claimed to have seen a ghost in the same cutter pick cabin that had no head, and he was so terrified he became hysterical and he had to be escorted out of the mine, and for some reason he didn't return underground for at least two years after that, and to this day he won't speak about it. The story of the headless man came about when a miner many years ago had stepped onto the shaft cage, but when on stepping onto it the cage suddenly dropped without warning and severed the poor man's head.

There was another story about four miners who were sent onto a level near the shaft side to repair an underground water dam and they were the only men working on that seam level that morning. They had to walk down a 100 yard long drift at an angle of about 25 degrees to get to this water dam which had to be repaired and built back up higher, because the existing top of the dam wall had crumbled away and it was now being breached by the mass of water behind it. This mine water was held back there until it could be pumped up in stages up the shaft and to the surface. Half way through the shift the work men saw another light shining down at them from the top of the drift, and on noticing it they shouted up the drift to find out who it was, but there was no answer and the light then just disappeared, but they all could hear the sound of footsteps walking over some corrugated tin sheets that they knew were scattered on the floor at the top of the drift, so the men assumed it was the pit deputy of that area just doing his rounds of inspection, and they just left it that.

On completion of the work and the walk back to the top of the drift they found that it was still a bit too early to ride out of the mine, so they decided to go into an old stables cabin to get out of the cold air ventilation coming down the shaft and kill the rest of the time in there. At the back of this cabin was a big steel door which was permanently padlocked shut and behind this door was a solid concrete block wall, which was put there many years before to seal off the old pony stables that were no longer used or ventilated by the mines air circulation, which meant it would be now full of deadly methane gas and carbon dioxide.

In the short time they rested they were sat merrily chatting amongst themselves, when all of a sudden they were all startled by a loud banging noise and it was heard coming from behind this permanently locked steel door, which was now moving and shaking with every bang that was made, and according to the story it sounded just like it was being hit with a sledge hammer from the other side, but later it was said by one of those men, it sounded more like when a pony would kick the stable door! Also the pit bottom deputy on that shift said he hadn't visited that area that day.

The ghost stories were numerous and at first on hearing them I thought that they perhaps were tales that were made up just to frighten the new recruits, but later on in my mining career I was to find out the truth of that for myself. (More ghost stories to come, stick around)

The 20 days of my close personal supervision with Dunk soon flew by because everything we did was varied and it all was new to me, which made my time all the more interesting and I've got to admit I had lots of laughs and a good old time, and the induction wasn't as bad as I thought it was going to be. After completion of my CPS I was fully trained at every mundane job in the Bot-Pittom there was and all that was left for me do was wait to see which one of those mundane jobs was picked for me?

These jobs being and starting in the order of the worst first, was the Greasing the Rails job: This job consisted of working at the back of the pit shaft where it entailed making sure all the empty tubs that were ejected from off the cage and sent down the rail track went without stopping, because the steel wheels of the tub would bind and sometimes get stuck on a tight bend in the steel track and it would cause others tubs to back up and stop the loading of full tubs onto the cage to go out of the pit. So the job was just to stand there constantly watering the tracks with a rag on a stick, applying a mixture of water and grease to the rails to make sure the tubs would run the length of the rail, otherwise it meant I would have to physically push them around for the entire shift.

The next job on from that was the Spiral loading chute loader, which was a spiral tube that went right up to the next level (The Nazi level) where a man sited at the bottom of it would pull a lever when an empty tub was exactly underneath to fill it to the brim with coal from the seam above. The next position after that was the Creeper chain and this was an endless chain that would automatically grab the tubs to take them up a short incline to the top, where another man would either couple the empty tubs together, ready to be pulled away by Loco and taken in-bye to be filled with coal from that particular seam, or send the full ones from the Spiral chute towards a steel roundabout that sent them back to the shaft side to go out of the pit to be emptied.

The most labour intensive job was the Lowering of the coal! This needed at least two or three men and it entailed lowering the full tubs of coal that were brought by the Locomotive from the stage loader in-bye where they had been filled. The loco would bring 36 tubs at a time from there, but it would leave half of them on a rail pass-bye and then it would return for the other 18 to be then steadily lowered into the pit bottom by the men using each of the tubs brakes to slow them down a steady incline towards the shaft side, ready to go up and out of the pit.

And the very last job on from that was just before the shaft side, where a man would stand uncoupling the tubs that was just lowered in to go onto the cage singularly. The only other position was the Onsetters job and he was the bloke who loaded all the tubs and men onto the cage, he was required to stand there the entire shift and hardly ever got a chance to have a break, but this job needed skill and required quite a bit of training to do, both practically and health and safety wise, so it wasn't a job a green kid like me was expected to do.

Although these jobs do sound pretty straight forward they all could be pretty dangerous as well, as I was later to find out. The first obvious point of danger was at shaft side where one could either fall down it or if you got your clothes accidentally snagged when loading the cage, you could easily be pulled up with it and then fall off higher up in the shaft. There was always the added risk of danger when stepping on to the cage outside of the riding times of it moving prematurely, this was because the deck safety stops wouldn't be in place to hold the cage firm, so there was always a possibility the cage could move up or down without warning, and this often happened if the pit top Winding house wheels brakes accidentally slipped, and like in some cases in the past, men were actually decapitated and even chopped in half.

There was also other types of danger, especially when heavy machinery and equipment that was too big to fit on the cage was instead slung underneath to be steadily lowered down the shaft, there was always the risk of the load breaking free, and when it did it was only within seconds of hearing the initial warnings on the tannoy system from above that the pit bottom staff usually managed to escape before tons of stuff came crashing down, causing massive damage to the Pit bottom area. There were also other items that fell down the shaft besides men and equipment, and this usually happened in some of the harsh winters we used to have, and when huge icicles of up to 10ft long and two foot wide at the thickest end would sometimes break off from somewhere higher up in the shaft, which had either formed when the ring dams had frozen over or a water pipe had burst in the shaft through the intense cold, and when they did they would suddenly come crashing down without warning and explode on impact as they hit the deck in the bottom, blasting the whole area with a layer of ice. The funny thing was when I first experienced this it took me by total surprise, I dove for cover thinking the whole pit bottom had blown up, only to hear this Convict 99 character the Onsetter, who was still stood in his position as cool as a cucumber, laughing at me and shouting "Cocktails anyone?"

It could be a bit dodgy at the back of the shaft too because there was always the possibility that someone could get run over by a speeding tub, especially if for some reason the

Onsetter had to eject a full tub from the cage, because its weight would give it too much momentum and it would go too fast on the track and on it striking the buffers of all the empty tubs that were waiting in line at the other end, it would have knocked them around like skittles, resulting in injuring or killing any unsuspecting man working in that vicinity. But you could say this about every place and work stage throughout the whole Bot-Pittom area, because everything was so confined and the only place of safety to run to in all cases was a man hole, and that's why there were lots of them. If the emergency siren sounded and no matter where you were in the pit bottom everyone ran for cover because it could only mean one thing, the emergency pull cord had been pulled by a locomotive driver and that meant trouble! His heavily loaded train of 36 tubs of coal were now speeding out of control towards a confined area which was full of empty tubs and workmen. (This happened a few times and men were killed) So this is why there was always care to site man holes at all the vulnerable places.

Another hazard which cost me at least two helmets, was on coupling and uncoupling the tubs with a coupling hook as they crashed buffer to buffer in line that were being pushed by the Creeper chain, because the gap between tubs was tight and there was barely enough room as it was and if the tubs happened to be the opposite way round, it meant the brake mechanisms of each tub would be adjacent leaving no room at all, and if you weren't paying enough attention or in a hurry, there was a good chance it would trap your head!

Officially a pit bottom man

So now I that was fully trained in all the fields of expertise, I was bestowed with my first ever title, a Pit Bottom man! And not only that I was actually classified as an adult miner too, whoopidoo! From that moment on the pit deputy wasted no time testing me out on each of the jobs to see which suited him the best? After couple weeks of doing so and when he was satisfied I was capable at them all, he then decided to deploy me to the Creeper chain on a regular basis. Little did I know at the time, that if you fitted in with everyone there and were actually capable of doing all the jobs, it was harder to get out and escape the Bot-Pittom!

So there I was stuck in this mundane job day after day in the freezing cold and praying every day for warmer weather to come, and as one can imagine after nearly getting my head crushed a couple of times the novelty of my new job started to wear off in a short space of time, so from then on the days grew longer and the weeks started to drag, and by the time I had reached my third month it was becoming all too obviously clear that the management had no intention of letting me work in-bye, and there I was meant me to stay.

Every day I would have to watch my mates climb in the empty coal tubs to go work in-bye, and each day without fail I would hear them all shout out "PETE MCGOWAN BOT-PITTOM" which was always followed by a loud cry of laughter from the tub they were sat in. Although the laughter was at my expense it was really funny, because they kept adding little variations to it each time they shouted it out, which multiplied the comedy affect. But as time went by this big joke between me and my mates also caught on with rest of the other young miners and it wasn't long before half the train was now joining in the joke, and although it was all just a bit of fun it was also a bit unnerving at the same time, especially when all my pit bottom buddies started to join in as well, which immediately reminded me of the last scene in the film Body Snatchers, when that lone surviving woman approaches Donald Sutherland for comfort thinking he was still a human being, but it turns out he wasn't and he then lets out this weird scream and then he points her out to the other aliens instead, who all start screeching and pointing at her too!

Another weird thing about this situation, and according to my Bot-Pittom workmates, the "PETE MCGOWAN, BOT-PITTOM" could still be heard coming from the riding tubs even when I was attending Whitwood Technical College or having day off, they still shouted it out regardless of whether I was there or not. After a while though, no matter how funny it originally was it started to grow a bit tiresome and wear a bit thin, it also occurred to me that not only was I trying to escape the Bot-Pittom, but I was also now trying to escape the big joke as well!

So until then I just had to laugh it off, none the less my reality still remained the same of being stuck there and I would have to watch my mates off every day heading in-bye to go and do a man's job, and at the end of it get a man's pay in return. It was soul destroying to hear them talk about the amount of wages they had received in their pay packets each week, which were double that of mine, and they would also often have discussion about buying things like a cars or motorbikes or even taking holidays abroad, and there was me living on the bread line and still having to go home and argue with my Mum over my pay packet (my Mum was still a bit hard up) about how much she wanted out of my pitiful wage and how much I could keep. From day one on receipt of my first earnings, my Mum was insistent that I had to tip up all my wage to her, and that she would give me pocket money when I needed it, (as if bless her haha) so as one can imagine the big arguments that followed before we eventually came to terms and we both settled on me giving her £7 board out of the usual £14.00 a week, but when she discovered I was now on a adult wage of a massive £22.00 she managed to squeeze it up to £10. Most of my workmates who on higher wages than me, paid around £5.00. There were some lads whose parents were better off than most and they paid no board at all!

It was very frustrating, no matter how much I pestered the training officers it fell on deaf ears, all they kept repeating was the same line every time, "I was needed there and that was that!"

So it looked like I was going to be stuck there in the Bot-Pittom for a quite a while, and it was a case of having to grin and bear it for the time being.

I was now resigned to my fate and just as I was thinking how the time was going to drag, when I did actually see a light at the end of the tunnel, and it was in the form of the head light of a diesel locomotive train that was coming towards the Bot-Pittom fully loaded with coal from in-bye. It was when I was asked to help lower in this run of coal tubs of two separate runs of 18 tubs to the shaft side, a particular Loco driver called Charlie who was a really nice bloke and he had heard of my displeasure of having to work there, and he asked me if I wanted to go Shunter/Guard training. Charlie was the head diesel locomotive driver who was in charge of all the other drivers and shunters, and he said that it was time I learnt to be a Shunter/Guardsman! To be truthful I think he took pity on me and he just wanted to show me around the rest of the mine, because there were no actual places available, but he argued the case to the deputy that I could be used as a spare Shunter when needed. So after that being settled he took me under his wing to complete the whole amount of training to be done with him.

While Shunter training I was to be under the supervision of Charlie's regular Shunter, who would keep an eye on me and show me the ropes of the job. The trouble was no matter how necessary this was, it also meant that now the two of us had to share the same hand and foot space that was available when we both had to ride on the back of the diesel locomotive, where there was barely enough room for one person. At first we used a special riding plate, but it was too impractical to lug it about from one end of the train to another all shift long, so it usually meant us sharing the same steel buffer of the loco to stand on and the steel head lamp casing to hold on with our hands, which sometimes was a struggle to hold on to, especially when we were travelling in areas of low roof where the supports were bent down with the weight of strata, which hardly left any room for the diesel to fit through at all, in these places we would have to crouch really low and practically squat down on our heels with only our toe ends barely on the loco's steel buffer, and because the rail track was usually uneven it made the locomotive jerk up and down and whip from side to side when we least expected it, which meant that half the time we would be just clinging on by our finger tips as well.

Sometimes it could be very dangerous because there was always the possibility of having a head on collision with another diesel that was coming around a bend, or if the track had shifted over night with the movement of the strata and the loco driver hadn't noticed it, the locomotive could clip the side of the roadway and cause it to derail! This happened quite often, I personally experienced this a couple of times.

Despite all the danger and the thrills and spills and nearly getting my head knocked off several times by not knowing when to duck, which usually resulted in me getting knocked off the loco and left lay.ing flat on my back in the track minus a hat, I really enjoyed the whole time, I just thought the added danger made it loads more fun. The best thing about it was not only did I get to see different places in-bye, but I also got to work where the air was warm for a change, and because we were always busy flying about on the loco the shifts seem to just fly by as well, which was a much welcomed break from being you know where!

I think the best memory of that total experience was sharing the company of Charlie the head loco driver because he was a larger than life sort of character who could make a person feel better in any given situation (everything felt more interesting in his company) and his most distinguishing feature was his absolutely perfect handlebar moustache, which he maintained and kept to a high standard because he often frequented the famous Good Old Days show at the variety theatre in Leeds!

Charlie was always full of stories and more often than not he would pull my leg with some of them so I never knew what he was telling me was actually true, and he always would say to me that if I was to ever meet a really nice young lady to settle down with, I had to promise to fetch her to visit him and he would open a big tin of Salmon which he kept on the top of the cupboard that he had been saving for a special occasion?

No sooner had I completed this Shunter/Guard training though, I was put straight back in my old position in the Bot-Pittom, which was a massive anticlimax and it instigated me to do something about it. So this time I decided to pay our union secretary a visit, who just happened to be another man called Charlie, but he was famously known throughout the British coal fields as one of the more moderate mouth pieces of the local branch officials of the NUM who held a certain amount of support, and because of this and when there was a potential crisis in the industry he was often called upon by local TV networks to express those moderate views, which in the long run gained him a lot of respect, not only from the union members but also management too, which in turn enabled him to gain more leverage when dealing with the management at that time. Whereas at some of the more militant pits they didn't seem to enjoy that same flexibility we had with our management, because they would generally work to rule. For example, at our pit we didn't stop work for snap time underground, so we got a better concessions regarding our riding times out the mine, also, if ever there was a dispute Charlie would say those famous words "Leave it to me", and instead of us all downing tools and walking out on strike, he got it sorted somehow, and for that reason Sharlston seemed to get a better deal than most other collieries! So I guess some liked him and some didn't, which is often the case in union politics.

So there's was me a 16yr old lad now stood in front of the giant of the union movement presenting him with my petty little case and half expecting to be fobbed off and ushered away to a lesser mortal, but after telling Charlie about my financial plight and overall personal circumstances at home, he was quite sympathetic and after our discussion he then stood up to shake my hand, and on parting company he actually repeated those famous words when he said, "leave it with me lad".

The very next day I was standing outside the Bot-Pittom office cabin expecting to hear my name called out by the deputy and followed by the dreaded Bot-Pittom attached to the end of it as usual, when this time the voice shouted "PETE MCGOWAN S2 CENTRE GATE SUPPLIES" instead. On everyone on hearing this there was a huge cheer of "HURRAY" let out from just about everyone stood in the vicinity, it felt as though everyone was actually happy for me (and to put into a more modern perspective of that feeling, it was just like in the film *The Truman Show* where the viewing public were all willing Truman on to escape and everyone was so happy when he actually did?) I couldn't have been any happier, especially on receiving all the pats on the back from my mates as I eagerly climbed into the tubs to finally join them at last! At that very moment I remember feeling so relieved and thinking that perhaps from now on I could be a proper miner and be able to fetch home a decent living wage.

The journey in-bye with my mates took about twenty five minutes in all, and after stopping at several locations to drop men off we came to a final halt at a place called the Lifting

Station. This was a big high junction of roadways splitting off in three different directions that was about 20 ft high with a traverse Crane attached to the underside of the girders above, which was used to make it easier to load and unload materials going to each of the districts, because each had their own pulley car supply systems that were independent of the main road rail track.

The Lifting Station was also a meeting place where men received their deployment at the start of the shift and it was here I again heard my name called out and I was told to go with a certain group of men, and one of these guys was to keep a close eye on me. This bloke was called Tommy or Neany to those who knew him, he was the nicest bloke you could ever wish to meet, who on introduction gave me a warm and friendly handshake and said reassuringly "Come on, thaz wi me kid", and then he told me I was to be with them full time from now on, which sounded good to me! We then set off walking in line with some other men who were also heading to that seam and about five minutes later we arrived at another form of transport and this was called a Cooley car (a series of flat bed train carriages with over and sideways wheels that kept it locked on the track, it was pulled by a endless rope that went the whole distance of the track which then returned around a giant pulley that was bolted to the ground at its final end. This allowed an endless loop of rope to go round in circles that was pulled by a mechanically driven drum).

We then climbed aboard this Cooley car which was sat waiting at the bottom of a steep drift that looked to go upward for hundreds of yards, it was impossible to see the top but only some distant lights. When the Cooley car guard assistant rang the overhead signal wire of 2 rings then another 2, it set off climbing up this steep drift, which I realised was about 200 metres long once we got to the top and where I was expecting to alight, but I was told by Neany to stop onboard because we had another three stops before it reached its final destination and where we were to get off.

Next we stopped at a new face development of the P2 district of the Birkwood seam, firstly at the main gate and then the tail gate. Our stop was next and right at the return end of the Cooley car pulley system. When we eventually arrived at the final stop there were only three of us left onboard, and the other guy was also working with us and his name was Frank who informed me we still had a couple of hundred metres of marching yet to go, "so we had better crack on" he said. When we got to my new place of work, which was the Nostel centre gate that supplied the farthest coal face in the mine the S2 district, the first thing we did was have some snap and a drink from a flask of tea that Neany quite was happy to share around, and as I slurped on his tea he explained that we should eat up all our snap now because wouldn't get a chance later. And he was right about that!

While we were having a bite to eat, Neany and Frank were explaining to me what the job actually entailed and how we were going to go about it, they also went on to tell me that all the other men on this coal face travelled from our pit to the adjacent Nostel Colliery by special coach, and that they descended the Nostel shaft because it was quicker going that way, which meant they would arrive on the district at least an hour before us, so they would be desperate for supplies, and we needed to take enough in-bye to last three coaling shifts.

By the time I had eaten every last crumb of my snap that my Mum had kindly made for me, I was fully informed of my duties and the three of us then set about loading five flat Cooley cars with timber of every length shape and description, all cut to measured lengths for each particular job on the coal face. We also loaded up lots of steel rings and these were the arch shaped girders that held the roof up, which came in three heavy sections consisting of two legs and a crown that bolted together with heavy forged arch shaped fish plates. There was a plethora of other mining equipment that had to be transported to the coal face and no matter what it was, the one thing all mining equipment had in common despite the outward appearance, it was always heavy.

When the train was as fully loaded as we dared to load it, I boarded the front where I was given the job of jumping off the Cooley cars while still moving so I could open the oncoming air doors, and Neany would ride on the back and close the sets of doors behind us (so not to short circuit the mines airflow system) while Frank stayed there to drive the big electric steel drum that pulled the rope to make the Cooley car run (This was called a Pickrose). Just before we set off Neany then surprised me when he said we needed to take all my gear with us because we might have to go out the pit another way, which I didn't understand at first, but it wasn't long before I found out why.

With the train now fully loaded Neany then pulled on the signal wire and gave the signal to Frank to set off, which was two rings then another two, and although Frank was just stood at the side of us and manning the Pickrose engine, the signal was still required for health and safety purposes in order to give those working in-bye a warning on their signal tannoy that the rope was about to move. The Cooley cars then set off at a steady 5mph, but it was still pretty exciting to me because I didn't know what to expect next. Each and every turn the Cooley cars made I saw something I hadn't seen before, it was especially interesting when we passed through some old roadways that had been previously flooded over the years before being eventually pumped out for re-use, which now had left all the roof supports and corrugated sheeting completely bright orange with rust. The Cooley car journey was about an hour in total and it wasn't until we had gone down two drifts and made at least two sharps turns in the track and passed through three sets of air doors, we eventually arrived at our destination of the S2 cross gate.

On arrival at the cross gate it was very noticeably hot and the air was thick with dust, and the scene there was a buzz of activity with big strapping lads that suddenly emerged from out of this dust cloud and headed in our direction, who then

Top: A Pickrose haulage engine.

Middle: Load transfer to Cooley Car.

Bottom: Belt roadway.

on first sight began to complain as to where we had been up until now, but it all turned out to be a bit of jest and bravado, because they knew how long journey it took to actually get there. In an instant everyone began hurriedly unloading the materials from our Cooley cars and straight onto the gate Cooley cars for the main and tail gates, because it turned out these supplies were urgently required. So we loaded them on the waiting Cooley car trams in record time ready to be taken straight to the coal face, no sooner we had and to my further surprise we were then told by the district supply deputy to take this load straight into the tail gate, because there had been a gate side roof collapse and the face men were desperate for timber!

With the two tail gate Cooley cars fully loaded up with these urgently needed supplies we both set off up the gate towards the awaiting face team in-bye, but this time with me walking at the front of the Cooley cars and Neany walking on the back, this was because the gates were not only uneven and we might get a derail, but also of the fact that riding on the gate Cooley cars was actually illegal. This was even more exciting to me because it was the first time I was actually going to see a coal face at Sharlston and where all the action was at last, I couldn't wait. However the journey was longer than I thought, because the S2 district was nearly at the end of its life and it had nearly advanced as far as it was going to go in this particular seam of coal, it was now around four thousand metres long and it would take at least another 25 minutes or so before we actually arrived at the coal face.

On our arrival at the coal face we were soon noticed, when the crisscrossing cap lamp beams we saw in the distant activity were now all focused in our direction and rapidly heading our way. Within seconds a large group of face workers descended on our supply train and began stripping it of everything they urgently needed to shore up the roof. Each man would grab a selected piece of timber as fast as he could, and then disappear back into this dusty din from where he came, and then suddenly reappear for another piece until both Cooley cars were completely emptied. No sooner they were Neany had already signalled the Pickrose driver three rings, followed by another three to go out-bye, and we set off again for another run of timber. So on that visit I didn't get a chance to have a good look around and see what was actually going on, because the airborne dust was too thick the visibility was down to about two yards, but I was still determined to have a right good old butchers on my next run!

On arriving at the end of the gate though, and while we were loading the next run up to go back in-bye, one of the other supply guys decided he was going to test my metal by instead of passing me the sacks of stone dust we were loading properly (these were cement bag size) he was acting big and being a bit cocky, and instead he began throwing them hard and fast and making sure they were hitting me high in the chest, it was as though he was trying to knock me on my arse for a laugh, which to be truthful was really tiring me out just to keep up with him, and although he was a lot bigger and stronger, I was determined he wasn't going to get the better of me and I had the attitude that I was going to show him!

Especially when I noticed that the under manager for the district had arrived on the scene, who was now stood there watching us all work, and for some reason he seemed to be watching me only, so noticing this I naturally tried to beef up my action at bit trying to impress him that I could do the job, however when I went to lift this big heavy hydraulic ram all by myself, and although I knew it was going to be really heavy, I was more than sure I could lift it, but I couldn't get a grip, it was covered in oil and too slippery to keep a hold of (oil and rubber gloves don't mix) so naturally it ended up dropping to the floor, and no sooner it hit the deck this under manager came rushing over towards me and physically pushed me aside to inspect this precious ram, and he then began meticulously checking it for any damage, luckily for me there wasn't any, but still this under manager insisted on making a load of noise and a right song and a dance about it, and he kept going on about "if it had got damaged," basically he went a bit over the top about it all. Although I was a bit scrawny then I had the heart of a lion and I always considered myself to be a good worker, so I didn't think a honest mistake would matter that much, after all it took two of us to load the ram in the end, but it struck me at the time that this under manager might not actually have been that bothered about dropping the hydraulic ram, but more so of Charlie the union secretary's intervention in overriding him to take his much needed man out of the Bot-Pittom and putting me there instead?

No sooner had myself and Neany loaded up the second run on the tailgate Cooley cars and strapped its cargo down tight with load locks chains the sudden appearance of the face men who were now arriving at the gate end meant it was time to go home, and this run would now have to wait for the afternoon shift. Neany then informed me that because the face team were travelling the Nostel colliery way out of the mine, they would be on time for their bus, but if we went out the way we came using the centre gate, we would definitely miss the diesel Manrider train back to the Sharlston pit bottom, so the only option he explained was to take an alternative route, but this alternative route actually turned out to be a journey to which I can only describe in a more up to date way was more like going on some kind of *Indiana Jones* type of adventure instead.

The Indiana Jones Adventure

The few of us that were left to make our way out the Sharlston way gathered up all our personal gear, and no sooner we had we then set off together walking in troop towards out-bye, but at a extraordinarily hurried pace, as it turned out that we were a bit late setting off due to the fact we had to stay on the job longer to load up the emergency supplies.

Firstly we went through a set of air doors that ran between the cross gate and into the main gate where the conveyor belt system began, and it was also where everyone jumped on to the moving conveyor. I just copied what they did (which was an illegal practice to do but everybody did it) and although this wasn't my first time riding on conveyor belts, the ones I had rode on before were proper man riding belts which were at the area training colliery, and they had boarding and alighting stations, whereas the belts we were riding on had none at all, and the only way of getting off these conveyors was to make a grab for a over head cable or a wire that was purposely tied in place by the illegal riders for that purpose, or whatever was available or you might end up going down a coal chute or even worse, into a lump crusher!

I remember we rode at least three different conveyor belts and one of them already had coal travelling on it, so it was necessary to level the coal out that peaked in the middle to make a space so that we could all lay flat, which was essential because there was quite a few low platform bridges that spanned the conveyor belt structure in many places that we had to pass under, which either held heavy electrical panels or ventilation fans, but some were just gangways to allow the

Cross Gate Cooley car track.

men to cross the conveyor belt. At one stage we rode under another chute that was still loading on from another conveyor and we all ended up getting covered with a layer of coal. The gangway catwalk bridges were lower down on the structure than the rest of the bridges and they were a really tight squeeze to get underneath, which made it necessary to lay flat as a pancake to get through. The very first one I went under both my helmet and lamp battery pack scraped hard on the bridge structure above as I passed through, and I was only a slender lad!

This is why fat blokes didn't ride the conveyor belts in many places underground, because if there was a few of these low platforms over the conveyor and someone who had a big arse attempted it, they would definitely get jammed underneath the structure, and the coal that was coming from behind would have backed up or probably end up going up the trouser legs and out the neck hole of that person until someone stopped the belt, and as funny as this may sound, this happened a few times! So all the big lads (fatties) and older miners with dodgy knees that couldn't ride the belts, were usually allowed under special circumstances to set off walking out-bye a bit earlier than the rest.

It was a bit unnerving at times, especially when we had to get off one particular conveyor belt that was one of the main belts that took the coal from a couple of the districts, because these had to run faster than the ones loading onto it, therefore it went twice the speed of an official man riding belt and they usually went higher off the ground, especially when they came to the underground coal bunkers where they would have to rise upwardly to go above the height of the bunker walls, which could be at least 10ft foot from the floor by the time we reached the place where we had to get off, and whereas all the other men knew all these places to grab a hold of something when that time came, I didn't it was just a case of follow my leader and copy exactly what the others did, no matter what!

Eventually we ran out of conveyors to ride and from then on it was a case of completing the rest of the journey on shank's pony (on foot) and in that time we had passed by a coal bunker, walked down a steep drift and gone through several sets of air doors, and after about twenty minutes of marching later we finally arrived at the lifting station, where a packed man riding train of men was already parked and waiting. They were waiting all right, waiting for us, and on everyone noticing our teams eventual arrival, we received a right load of abuse for being late, just about half the train was shouting "WHERE THE FUCK HAVE YOU BEEN!" and other similar nasty things, while purposely shining their light beams in our faces to see who it was who dared to hold up the manrider train at home time.

No sooner had we late comers found ourselves a space in a tub, the train suddenly set off without any warning at all, no whistle, none of the usual formality it just set off, yanking all the tubs and the passengers necks with it as it accelerated straight into its top speed towards the pit bottom, which was a clear indication to all onboard that the Loco driver was going to make up lost time no matter what, and it was going to be a faster than normal ride out of the mine!

Which was all well and good, I certainly didn't want to be late out of the pit, but for the sake of a few minutes I still didn't fancy getting killed in the process either. Under other circumstances I would have normally drawn comfort from the fact that none of the other passengers sharing my tub showed no concern at all, which should have been enough to reassure me that everything was quite normal and ok, but on this occasion and despite being still a bit green and wet behind the ears, I felt I knew better and their lack of concern was only because they didn't know something that I knew. Which was something I had learnt only recently when I was doing my stint of Shunter/Guard training, and that was not only did I know where all the bad stretches of the track where and where all the derailments had occurred in the past, but I also knew that this particular diesel driver was involved in most of those derailments I had heard of, and all the other diesel drivers and pit bottom staff thought this driver was a bit of a risk taker and was quite mad!

So every time we came to places where I knew the track was a bit dodgy, instead of being relaxed like everyone else, I was bracing for a crash and ready to bail out at any second. (It felt like I was the only passenger on a aeroplane that knew there was a bomb on board!) And no matter how fast the train went or how much we all got jiggled about like potatoes in a sorting machine, no one else seemed to care, they were just sat on their helmets with their eyes closed dozing and rocking from side to side with the movement of the tub, just content to be heading home. (it reminded me of a typical scene in a Vietnam war film when the GI grunts were flown into battle riding in a Huey Helicopters, and while all veterans were all cool about it and dozing away sat on their helmets, the cherries would still be wearing theirs and nervously awaiting the unexpected).

Regardless of being jostled about in an unexpectedly mad train journey, I still had at least 20 minutes or so to rest up from the *Indiana Jones* adventure experience, because it was vital to preserved as much energy as I could for the next big hurdle that was still yet to come! And this hurdle was something I had heard about many times before, but never witnessed or participated in it due to the fact that by the time the in-bye lot entered the pit bottom area, I was already in the pit showers before it took place! So this was going to be my first time I was going to compete in The Stampede!

The Stampede

This took place when the man riding train was approaching the Bot-Pittom, and before the train came to its final halt, the men would jump from the moving train and run as fast as they could to get to the front of the queue to ride out the pit. As the difference between first and last man out the pit could be sometimes at least half hour!

We were soon nearing the Bot-Pittom and those who were going to run in the Stampede got up from sitting on their helmets and started getting prepared to alight. This was done by sitting on the brim of the tub with both legs straggling over the side (just like one would do riding on the back of a Waltzer car) and getting into a position they could easily jump off and run like the clappers to the bottom. So I just copied what everyone else did and sat on the side of the tub, but when the train went into the last bend it whipped us around so hard, I nearly fell back in the tub again, luckily I managed hold on by a bum cheek and keep my position long enough until we hit the final home straight and into view of the Bot-Pittom lights, and just as the locomotive train was slowing down, but still at least 50 yards from where it was supposed to come to its proper halt, the first of the men were already jumping off and running like crazy toward the pit bottom.

I managed to land with my feet running just at the right speed and being a natural runner I got a flying start and was off like the clappers too. It was just like being in the Grand National but more hazardous, instead of jumps and ditches we had to dodge parked diesels, tubs, and crisscrossing rails and track sleepers under foot. The air instantly became thick with dust that was either being kicked up from the floor or coming from the miners' clothing as they battled the oncoming cold wind that was coming down the mine, not to mention from those who had actually fell and bit the dust!

At the front of the race it was about five men deep, all desperately trying to aim for the same narrow passage that lead to the tunnel and the Pen, all hoping to make the first rope of men up the shaft, which was a necessity for me because I had to catch the 181 bus home, so I needed to get out early, besides that the other advantages maintaining a lead at the front of the Stampede was that you didn't have to eat everyone else's dust, not only that if you didn't make it to the front and into the holding Pen, it meant you would have to queue in a small narrow passage that was only two people wide with hardly any headroom at all, and when it was crammed full of men there was hardly any air to breath, so it usually stunk of a mixture of manky clothes, bad breath, sweat, foot odour, tobacco juice spit, snuff, piss and farts! Not a nice environment for a young lad who hadn't quite lost his sense of smell yet!

The Pen was a rectangular shaped cage that was very similar to a dog run and its mesh walls were about 6ft high which held about 50 men, and at the shaft end of it was the front of the queue, where it had a gate that had only to be opened by an official to make sure the men were let out in single file only to safely board the cage (well in theory that was supposed to happen, but in reality there was always a bit of pushing) The officials however, deputies and over men and management were afforded the luxury of walking straight to the front of the queue because their excuse was they had reports to take to the office, the very same one they had already phoned in from underground?

The Stampede was like a mad death race ritual that played out daily on every shift, but it was the cause of quite a few injuries over the years, and no matter how much the management tried to put an end to it they couldn't unless they were personally prepared to be present every shift to stop it by dishing out fines, which they did on the odd occasion, especially after someone got injured. The pit deputies and over men sometimes tried but they usually got half trampled to death in the process, and besides they could hardly issue fines to someone if they boozed in the same pub or club on a weekends, or they were near neighbours, so it was useless to try and stop it, so it became the norm.

The Stampede was a necessity for some, but it was like a competition to others, who were the type of people who took pride in winning everything, which made the front of the race quite interesting at times. Runners would do absolutely anything to get in front of each other, especially if they were racing against mates, which would often result in two lads running for the same narrow passage and one purposely nudging the other down the wrong path and sending them off course into a obstacle or dead end, or they would even try to trip each other up by kicking each other's ankles, and sometimes they would even go as far as elbowing a competitor in the face to get in front. And if someone fell no one stopped, it was a dog eat dog mentality, and on hearing the painful moans and groans of someone that had tripped and bit the dust, instead of them getting any sympathy, all they would hear would be jeers of laughter instead, it was brutal but a good laugh.

Within seconds the tiny passage and Pen would be full to the brim and the queue of men would trail right back up the small drift of the Creeper chain. (The very same Creeper chain that was my regular job only the shift before) There would be about two hundred men in the queue, usually with all the younger lads at the front and the older or slower ones at the back, and there was always a contingent of craftsmen who would be hanging at the back to sneak an hour over time on the pit top too, *shhhh!* Whereas the older generations would queue in an orderly fashion the young ones in the Pen would be pushing and shoving and swaying about like they were on the football terraces and would be either singing or just shouting obscenities and hurling abuse at each other, sometimes there was even the odd fight!

It used to get particularly rowdy behind the pen especially when on the odd occasion someone who wasn't entitled, but was hard faced enough to dare to walk straight into the pit bottom and to the front of the queue. It was accepted that management and officials and diesel drivers, Shunters and pit bottom staff were justified, even the union officials observed this protocol, so it was a case of woe betide anyone else who tries to push in, and those who did try could expect to receive the most hateful scorn and abuse, and if the mob became angry enough there were even threats of violence. But then again that depended who it was, if it was a big tough bloke, a bit of a gripper that might just give you a slap in the lockers, you would barely hear a disgruntled murmur. Funny that, innit?

When the shaft side signal bell rang 4 rings followed by another 4, no matter where you were in the queue you would know by the cry of cheers from the lads at the front that would travel down the line of men, and everybody would soon know it was riding time. The Pen would be opened slightly to let the men out in single file to board one of the three decks of the cage, which lifted up one deck at a time. Each deck was rammed full over capacity (the capacity for each deck was 17 men, but that was for going down the mine, going out we had different rules) The men were so tightly packed on the cage that it was usual for the last ones on to be assisted on by the sole of the Onsetters boot, so he could finally lower the concertina gate that held them on.

For my first Stampede I didn't do bad at all and I made it near to the front of the queue in the Pen, but it still didn't guarantee me a place on the first rope out the mine, this was because the first two decks were usually taken up by colliery officials and diesel drivers and Shunters etc, so it looked like yet another desperate scramble to actually get on the last remaining deck, and this was when I expected the real pushing and shoving to start, because everyone near the front would look at the last spaces available on the cage and do their own mental head count to see if they would fit on, so the men just behind me in the queue would be more desperate and some of them were big blokes and ex rugby players etc., so they would be pushing hard from the back to make sure that they did.

When it came the time for the pit bottom deputy to open the Pen, I got ready for a bit of a scramble and prepared myself to use everything necessary to make sure I didn't lose my place, elbows and toe nails as they say! Fortunately for me the sudden surge of the men from behind practically lifted me up off my feet and carried me straight onto the cage with no effort at all, however the force that picked me up and carried me on also slammed me forward into the back of the bloke in front, which just about squeezed every last bit of air out my lungs in the process, and before I barely had time to fill them up again, another sudden surge came from behind to empty them again when the last man was forced on by the Onsetters boot (The lesson to be learnt there was to always brace with your arms forward on shoulders of the man in front until loading was complete).

When the safety gate was then finally dropped shut the Onsetter rapped to signal for the cage to go, within a few seconds the cage began to lift upwards, in that instant there was an unanimous sigh of relief that could be heard coming from all on the three packed decks of the cage as we all headed up the shaft, and because there was no need to be braced for any pushing or shoving everyone eased off a bit and it made much more room on the deck, with each man now resting his elbows or chin on the man in front and the atmosphere became much happier, and practically cheek to cheek and chewing tobacco in the next miner's ear hole the daily banter and piss take began.

I remember feeling very much at home in this type of humour and atmosphere, so joining in the fun was pretty easy for me, and for the first time I was actually beginning to feel like one of the lads!

The icing on the cake which made that whole days experience special was when we were just breaking the surface daylight and a voice from the bank shouted a message down the shaft intended for his mate he knew would be on board the cage coming up, which was answered by his mate with a near perfect Tarzan call in response! (Who was that bloke?) It made the hairs prickle up on the back of my neck it was so good. The cage finally halted at the bank side on the surface and because we were the last to get on the lower deck, it meant that we were to be the last off, so the while each deck was emptied of men in turn, we would be left dangling at the low landing where the cold air was pulled down the shaft at ground level, and if anyone's under clothes were already wet through with sweat, it would suddenly become freezing cold on their skin, and because mine were and I was a bit skinny, I was shivering with the cold and counting down the seconds.

When it became our turn we were hoisted up to the bank level the awaiting Banksman swiftly lifted up the deck gate to let us off, which was a task he had probably performed thousands of times before, and regardless of it being a first for me to ride the shaft at shift time with the rest of men, when I stepped from the cage and handed him my brass check in full view of the long queue of the entire afternoon shift who were waiting there to go down the mine, I was black as the ace of spades and indistinguishable from everyone else, and at that moment I distinctly remember feeling so proud that my chest grew by at least another four inches as I walked past them all, I actually felt like a proper miner!

Making the experience even more memorable was when our warm breaths first hit the still cold air of the bank side which turned to white steam that instantly reminded me of the Freddie Truman advert on TV, where he is seen coming out of a coal mine and when the Banksman lifts the cage gate he breaths out the cold air, but later in the pub after drinking Webster's Pennine bitter he breaths out a flame, so with that in mind it was exactly what I intended to do as soon as I got home to my local Working Men's Club, but without the flames though.

Although the underground stampede was behind us the race wasn't quite over yet, there was still more hurdles to cross. There was another mad dash to the lamp room to return our lamp and self rescuer and site them properly back in the correct holders, then there was another 50 yard dash to the pit baths to get undressed as quickly as I could, followed by another desperate dash to try and find a decent shower that actually worked properly.

Luckily I managed to grab a good shower cubical straight away, within seconds I was happily soaping myself down and as quick as I could, when all of a sudden I felt this solid heavy thud in the centre of my back, which launched me forwards and nearly splattered me into the white tiles in front. When I turned around to see who it was, I saw the biggest hairiest bloke I've ever seen in my life, who then impatiently said "come on lad knock about, duz tha want thi back weshing or what", then without waiting for a reply he physically spun me around again and just began scrubbing my back with this big giant sponge, but he was really heavy handed about it, he seemed to be knocking me all over the place purposely to show how feeble I was (I think it was a masculine thing, but I couldn't help thinking at the time that it was exactly how I imagined a prison shower rape scene would begin) when he had finished he then turned his back around for me to do the same to him. His back was huge it looked like what I imagined a Bigfoot's back would look like, it was about four feet wide and completely covered in thick black hair, and because I was too scared of offending him by asking to use his sponge, and also the fact I didn't have a zoo keeper's hat, wellies, hosepipe and sweeping brush to hand, it left me no choice but to complete this grizzly task by using my brand spanking new Loofah that I hadn't even had a chance to use yet, and if that wasn't bad enough, when I'd finished scrubbing this Bigfoot down and he had left me and gone back to his own shower cubicle (cave) he had also had left me with half his body hair trapped in my Loofah, which I daren't use until every last one was extracted. By the time I managed to get showered and dressed and make it outside the canteen entrance the bus was already at the stop and nearly ready to leave, fortunately there was someone still paying to get on with cat in a basket that delayed its departure, so you could say through a man's body hair I nearly missed a bus, but by a cats whisker I managed to catch it!

It was a good job really it was absolutely banging it down with cold rainy sleet outside, and if I missed this there wasn't one for another hour, which then meant going home on foot and that was about three and a half miles by the road way or two mile across the muddy fields, but if the miserable farmer had decided to plough the footpath up like he usually did, it felt more like ten miles instead.

Sometimes if you were popular or lucky you might even be offered a lift by someone who owned a car, but the truth was that some people were just too mean to offer you a lift and had a poor attitude towards others. I often heard some say "if they want to get home they should save up and buy a car like me, I'm not going to be someone's chauffer" etc., which I could sort of understand, but when blokes I knew well drove past me it did make me wonder about our friendship.

By the time I finally managed to sit down on the bus I was so completely and utterly drained of all my energy, I practically fell into my seat like I was made of lead. It felt such of a relief just to be finally able to sit down and have a rest, I was totally done in, but it wasn't because of the fact that I had to get up at stupid o-clock in the morning (4.30 am) or the fact I had worked a gruelling shift, it was actually the *Indiana Jones* type of experience and everything since just to make my way out the mine that actually did me in!

When the bus finally set off and I was secure in the knowledge I could finally relax, I took the time to notice the other passengers that were onboard, and in doing so it immediately struck me that most of them wouldn't have had the slightest inclination of this other world that I had only just emerged from that existed virtually beneath their very own feet, by way of a hole in the ground not more than hundred metres away from the road side, and all the effort it had taken me just to be sat there with them on this dammed 181 bus home.

Despite all the hardship though, and taking into account that If I had still been working in the Bot-Pittom I would be able to walk straight onto the cage with no fuss at all, get showered and dressed in comfort and even have time to have a cuppa in the canteen and still be in time to catch the bus, also taking into consideration that from now on I would have to repeat this performance every day just to get home, I still wouldn't have swapped places for all the tea in China as they say! I was enjoying my new job and for the first time I was really looking forward to going back to work.

That first week in my new job working in-bye on supplies seemed to just fly by, because once again everything was all new and still pretty exciting to me at the time, as you would expect it to be to a young lad, and although we were always kept busy and we had to work hard, we always managed to be able to have a good laugh, which like everyone knows makes time pass quicker, but another major reason was that we weren't actually on the job the whole shift, because it took an hour at each end just to actually travel to the district and back.

And it was the back bit I liked the best, I think it was the camaraderie we had in the way we all illegally travelled out the mine together, it felt a bit mischievous and like we were all naughty boys in a gang, and because there was always that added element of risk of danger of having a mishap, it made it a lot more exciting.

When the following Monday came and once again I boarded the man rider train and climbed into the tubs with my mates as usual, but as the train was just about to set off in-bye, I heard my name called out by the deputy and to my horror it had Bot-Pittom attached to the end of it again? I was gob smacked and looked at my mates in total puzzlement, only see the exact look on their faces looking at me, so instead of climbing out the tub to see what it was all about, I chose to ignore it, but I couldn't the Bot-Pittom deputy was insistent, he even began searching in all the tubs looking for me, and noticing this I decided to hunker down with my cap over my face and keep quiet and waited until the train set off. Soon I was alighting the Manrider at the Lifting Station and made my way to the deployment deputy as normal and really hoping whatever they wanted me in the Bot-Pittom for was handed down to some other sucker and I would be allowed to proceed to my new job. But that wasn't to be, to my absolute disbelief this deputy told me I had to report back to the pit bottom straight away! Neany and Frank looked at me in total surprise and they didn't know what to make of it, and neither did I?

When I reached the dreaded Bot-Pittom the deputy was already stood waiting for me as I exited the train, where he then informed me that in future I had to check with him first before going in-bye again. I couldn't believe it, "why is this happening to me" I thought? The deputy went on to tell me the reason why the under manager had specifically requested me was that he had seen how good of a job I had done when white washing walls in the pit bottom on a past occasion, and his story was that someone important was coming and he needed me to white wash the entire pit bottom? I didn't believe this for one moment, it immediately sprung to my mind that he had made his mind up when he saw me drop the slippery hydraulic leg the week before, and perhaps he thought I wasn't strong enough? Totally unaware that I had already worked very hard to rush supplies the tail gate, all these things were going through my mind, but it also occurred to me that it was more likely he didn't like being over ruled by Charlie the union secretary? What I couldn't believe was the Herculean task this under manager had actually thought up just for me, my heart sunk to my stomach and I felt gutted on hearing this news, the whole pit bottom he said!

The pit bottom consisted of a pit shaft with a road way at two sides each heading in opposite directions, one looped around to meet the other again in the shape of the small case of the letter (d) and all meeting with big high junctions which also had to be painted too. I had to do the area from the from the shaft side, which was about 20 feet high and about 30 feet wide supported with big steel girders, all closed in with either timber or brick, and all the road ways that tapered off from there were supported by steel arches which were usually closed in by corrugated sheeting and they were usually about 12 foot high by 15 feet wide. They stretched from the pit bottom area onward for about 100 metres, and the whole pit bottom area was in total about three hundred meter long. I was then informed I not only had to white wash it, but I also had to sweep it all down to remove the black coal dust that had accumulated over years before I started, which I estimated would take at least two weeks just to do that, even before I could even start mixing the white wash and begin painting it. As far as I was concerned at this point they might as well have told me to paint the Severn Bridge by myself, it was just as daunting a task. So now I was stuck in the Bot-Pittom again doing what I can honestly describe as the worst job in the world, all on my own for what looked like it was going to take a lifetime to do.

Day after day all through the rest of winter I was expected to do that job in the freezing wind, which I did at first conscientiously, but after a while of daily inspections by this under manager and having to listen to his patronising tone of approval I began to feel a bit of lacklustre in this type of work and was beginning to feel that there was no hope. So It wasn't long before I began to lose all interest in the pit and it wasn't long either before I started getting buzzed for work (sleeping in) and no matter how many alarm clocks I got or knives and forks I put on the metal tray I sat the clocks on, getting up on time got harder by the day, resulting in me having to request permission to come on the afternoon shift a few times.

Which fortunately turned out to be a good move, the afternoon Overman asked me what job I did and as a result he sent me in-bye on supplies and on the better money. Then one day after I had been making a bit of a habit of doing this, the under manager called me in to the office to ask me why I kept getting Buzzed for work? I can't remember the excuse I gave him but the end result was that he put me on regular afternoons as a punishment, not realising I actually preferred it, but his decision did make me wonder about this mysterious visitor that was supposed to be coming and his reason he tied me there in the first place? For that month I was on regular afternoons but doing a better job and in the warm air and liking it, but it passed too quick for me, when on the last Friday I was told to return onto the day shift again the first thing Monday morning and back in the Bot-Pittom.

So it looked like it was there I was meant to stay and there would be no escaping the long shifts and the mundane work and the dull atmosphere, which I knew was going to feel like an eternity, especially after working in-bye with the lads, not to mention the lower wages, it was a very depressing thought, so I started looking for jobs outside the mining industry, I was even considering going to work on the railways, where I actually managed to pass an interview, but just as I was on the verge of leaving Sharlston forever to go to this other industry, when to my big surprise we got two new recruits for the pit-bottom, each wearing brand new shiny yellow helmets (we got fresh meat!) At last I could see a means to an end, it was my big chance to escape forever and the management had no excuse to keep me there now I thought. So that day on coming out of the mine I went straight to see training officer, who on my previous visits had said that it was essential for me to work in the pit bottom, but this time because of these potential replacements they no longer had an excuse or argument to keep me there and now they agreed that there was no reason why I couldn't go back in-bye to the job on supplies, but with the understanding that I had to wait until the new recruits had finished their 20 days close personal supervision first, which I thought was fair enough.

So after another 4 week I was to be let free of the Bot-Pittom at last, but once again just as that month was over the same under manager called me into the office again. This time he wanted to know why I kept missing work every Monday, which sounded a bit odd to me and it automatically made me wonder "what is this bloke up to now?" Because he knew exactly why I was absent, and when I reminded him that I was attending technical college because I wanted to become a colliery manager, he pulled a face and then sneeringly replied "well you want to make your mind up you either want to be a miner working for me on supplies or a manager, which is it to be?" he snapped, meaning if I wanted the job on supplies I had to be there five days a week or otherwise you can guess where I would end up? So being desperate for the money I had no other choice, because the union would hardly fight my case to be a manager, it was like I was jumping ship to the other side, so the end result was that I decided to give up my technical college work, and take the full time job on supplies in-bye instead. (This was the reason why I didn't witness the Sam incident at the Technical College gym!)

The strangest thing about this whole experience was that the important person who was supposed to be coming and the reason for the white washing in the first place, never came! So I only ever referred to this under manager as Mr Cockhead from that day forth.

When my next shift came I was as pleased as Punch as they say to be back on supplies with my old muckers Neany and Frank on the Nostel centre gate, and where I stayed for a few more weeks, but just as I got settled into the routine again I was redeployed to work further in-bye to supply in both gates of the S2 coal face on a regular basis, which meant I was now required to travel on the pit bus to go down Nostel pit end to our workings along with the face team. It was a good move; we nearly always beat the riders coming out the Sharlston end to the showers!

At the Nostel pit end we could travel both of their shafts, but usually we went down what was called a Monkey shaft, which was probably named because it was small and there was only enough room for a monkey I reckon, otherwise I haven't a clue why. In fact this Monkey shaft cage rode seven men in total, and sometimes this shafts pit bottom would get flooded, and if the barometer was low on the surface, it was also prone to getting gassed off as well! So we often got diverted to make our way out the mine the Sharlston way.

We had quite a few incidents in that area, some were touch and go as to whether we would save the mine or not. One time it was a flood another time we had a fire in the old workings caused by spontaneous combustion, which was really serious, we all worked day and night with as much over time as we wanted, sealing off old workings and diverting the air flow to starve the fire of oxygen. The mine was buzzing with officials from all over the country, it even made the national and local news on TV, it was a tense situation and despite being constantly aware that we could all die at any moment, it was all very exciting at the same time (when you've been in mining for a few years you get used to things like this).

On another occasion the cage in the monkey shaft lowered the men into the pit bottom that they didn't know was flooded up to chest height and when the cage touched down a big column of water gushed through the hole in the cage floor and nearly frightening the men to death because they thought they were going to be drowned. The funny thing about this incident was that twelve of the men went home with shock hoping to get full day's pay, but that cage they rode was only supposed to hold seven men, so as one can imagine it instigated a bit of an investigation by the colliery manager and the head of the safety department.

In a later flood in the Nostel pit bottom the water was coming in so fast that the pumps in place were easily being overwhelmed by the incoming water, which meant there was more coming in than going out, and at a rapid pace too, it got so out of control the water was now running down a steep 1 in 1 drift and flooding into the Sharlston workings of the mine. The water was running over the edge at least six inch deep and it was just like a waterfall as the water turned white when it crashed at the bottom of the drift. The situation got so desperate that under the instruction the area manager every spare pump in Britain was sought. Some of our roadways at the bottom of the drift that linked the two mines became so flooded from this incursion that the swilly's (hidden dips) of these gates were completely submerged under water.

On one of these days I was working on sand bagging duties of this flood, and I remember seeing two electricians who had stripped off to dive under water to get to some vital equipment or get to an essential place for some reason. At the time I was filling sand bags to stop the water flooding towards the coal face and at the opposite end of this flooded gate, when I saw this guy suddenly emerged from out of this black water, at first I didn't know what to make of it at all, I was just stunned at the sight, I didn't know whether to run or hit him over the head with the shovel, that is until he actually spoke to me, and it turned out to be one of these mad electricians who was called Neil, he was diving under water for some reason and I think my first words to him at the time went something like "what the fucking hell are you doing, you nearly scared me to death you mad twat!" (Probably worse actually, I had a canny knack for swearing.....still have!).

There was another incident at the Nostel end which developed out of a usual occurrence, and this was when we got a message from surface control over the tannoys while we were on the district that informed us that the pit bottom we had travelled from was getting gassed off by the hour, and soon it was going to be closed off until the barometers mercury rose again on the pit top (low air pressure allows methane gas to seep out of the coal and rock to take the easiest route) So the officials of the district decided to send four of the men back to the Nostel pit bottom to recover the men's coats and belongings before it was completely gassed off. (so they could travel out the Sharlston end with their stuff). I can distinctly remember one of the officials asking one of those who were sent for the men's things to check the coats when he got there to make sure his glasses were in a certain coat pocket because he couldn't find them anywhere else and hoped he hadn't lost them. There were about twenty coats in all, so it wasn't going to be an easy job to carry them about a mile and a half in those hot sticky conditions, with drifts to climb and low girders to stoop under, so I wouldn't have relished that journey, regardless of the old saying "while thaz marching thy int fating".

When they did eventually arrive back at the district with everyone's jackets and the snap the men had left for the ride home on the bus, it was noticeable there was a look of concern on the faces of those who were sent to retrieve the coats. It turned out that the man who was asked to search the coats for some eye glasses had inadvertently found a box of matches, a couple of different types of cigarettes and a five pack of dark cigarillo's which was a distinctive brand that could only belong to one person there, and he was an official, the other smoking paraphernalia could have belonged to anyone else, but I reckon those who searched the coats knew exactly who the other culprits were.

This was contraband in the highest capacity, one naked flame or warm spark in gassy areas could have blown the whole two mines up, killing everyone. Of course because it was a big honcho on the team it was all conveniently hushed up and no one said a word about it and everyone stayed loyal, but if it had been someone like me I would have been vilified and sacked and would have probably had to move town in shame of all the gossip.

To tell you the truth I was ok with it, because I didn't think for one minute any of them were actually smoking down the pit, although I believe they were guilty of knowingly fetching them down the mine, I felt they just did it for a petty reason and they thought they would never be questioned or caught. The reason they did this was because it was known to us all who travelled the Nostel way out and especially smokers like me, we always fancied a cigarette on first hitting the surface before the coach came, so we would have to hide our cigarettes on the Nostel pit top for when we got out. The trouble was that the Nostel men would sometimes see us hiding our cigs or even go looking for them and nick our stash when we had gone underground, so we all knew why they had done it, but it didn't excuse them either, but I believe the incident worked out for the better in the end because the official in question was constantly aware that we all knew his big sack-able secret, so it gave us all a sort of get out of jail free card if needed in the future (if thanoz worra mean) but no one ever had to cash it in, because ever since that incident this guy became much more humble and more forgiving and less likely to be a jobsworth from that day on!

Looking back to those days I remember getting searched for contraband lots of times before going underground, which beside smoking materials included such things as silver paper, glass, and anything that gave off toxic vapours and alcohol etc. There was a right kafuffle one day when some bright spark reported finding cigarette tab ends in some empty coal tubs underground, which were obviously flicked inside while they had been on the pit surface, but the safety department went over the top about it, resulting in everyone getting searched before going down the mine for quite a while after that, it was made a serious matter and we were all told to stay very vigilant!

When S2's district eventually came to an end we were all moved onto the next coal face that was already developed ready and waiting and this was the P2 development which I had passed by on my first shift working in-bye. On this new district my job was to take the supplies in the main gate right up to the coal face, but I wasn't attached to any particular face team because they did three shifts and I was still under 18yrs, which meant I could remained on the dayshift, and this also meant I got to know all the three shifts face teams and all their differences and peculiarities. After a while it became noticeable to me who had the nicer characters of men and officials on each shift, so it was only natural I would prefer one team to another, and this was useful to know for any placement choices in the future.

A face team on an advanced face (an advanced face consisted of two road ways that were around 250 yards apart and when they advanced parallel together the coal that was in between would be extracted as they followed that particular seam of coal) usually consisted of Rippers, Waste men, and Machine men that cut the coal, there would be an Over man and two Deputies, one in each of the two gates, and other auxiliary workers such as Craftsmen (fitters and electricians) and a Chock fitter. Supporting them were coal Transfer point and Belt men, and supply teams that usually consisted of about three men who had their own gate end deputies to oversee their work and drive them on to make sure the gates were always supplied.

Some deputies were ok and would lend a hand, whereas others remained as clean as they entered the mine with absolutely no intention of giving anyone a hand with the work at all, and they would advertise their unwillingness to help by not tying their cap lamp cables on their helmets properly or they'd hold it in their hand instead to make it look like doing work would be awkward for them to do. Some deputies would help out but others used the generic off the shelf of convenient excuses, such as they weren't allowed to help or they'd say "I've done my day's working, it's thy turn naa"!

We supply men were always black and drip wet through with sweat and although I didn't mind the graft, what used to really annoy me was when we used to come across a certain slave driver deputy who always insisted that we did more than our fair share, keeping us busy right to the very last minute on the job to make sure he got every piece of work out of us before we could set off to catch the Manrider to go out the pit. What was particularly annoying about this bloke was when we happen to overhear this still very clean deputy giving his report to the under manager on the pit top, that went something like this: "I've done this boss, I've done that boss, I got this and that up the gate, blah, blah", the funny thing was he used to break out in a sweat describing all the work he had done. I didn't like working under him at all, it was soul destroying listening to him take credit while he never afforded us any, and he was my close neighbour! (I did use to kick my football in his garden a lot when I was a kid though).

Then a twist of luck came when I was put on a two shifts system of days and afternoons, which enabled me to shed this slave driver for a nicer deputy instead, who we nick-named Danbo. He was young and he seemed to be a part of this new breed of officials who were a bit flash and typically played golf, and he was an outgoing and charismatic sort of bloke who always spoke with a hint of sarcasm in his voice, which would wind a lot of people up but I liked him because I thought he was quite funny, and he liked to have a laugh as well, and if the going got tough he would always give us a hand, which brought the best out in us naturally.

It wasn't just the staff or management that could be twats, some of the men on the face teams could be as well. On one particular occasion me and a few supply lads along with the face team were sat at the end of the gate and all waiting for the Cooley car Manrider that took us down to the other seam towards the Lifting station, when I noticed this older gentleman looking me and a couple of my young work buddies up and down, but he was also very rudely shining his cap lamp directly in our eyes. When I heard him comment to his captive audience there, "Just look at these young lads here, they're nearly on as much money as us these lot", he said begrudgingly, then he added, "we ought to get paid on how long we have been here and on our age", he said authoritatively and in a matter of fact tone. Which I thought was the most stupidest thing I had ever heard, although I was young and a bit naive I was still fairly sure that his opinion contradicted our union's policy, in the knowledge that it took decades of union struggle and strife to get those very pay structures we had at that present moment in time, which guaranteed to everyone that from a certain age, that if they did a man's job they got a man's wage, but what made his statement sound even more stupid was the fact that he was a key Union representative at Sharlston Colliery. (Little did I know at the time how commonplace these contradictions of union policy were to become in the later years. I won't mention his name, but I can only describe him as old and he wore glasses and an old style eggshell style helmet and his bodily features outside his overalls looked like what I can imagine a Tortoise would look like if it was pulled from out of its shell.)

The P2 seam soon ran out of coal to mine and the men were then sent onto the E2 district of the same Birkwood seam, although that being the case, I was transferred down to Warren house seam, and this district was taking the coal from underneath the worked out Birkwood seam above and the old worked out Barnsley seam that was below it, which made the strata very unstable, making conditions worse than normal. This was because the supporting rock above the coal was weak shale which easily fragmented and was always loose. One particular day I was put on a coal transfer point (Button job) on the Warren house 21s main gate, and this job merely entailed watching the coal load from one conveyor to a steel panzer chain that took it to another conveyor, to make sure that great big lumps of coal or rock didn't get stuck in the conveyor chute, or else a pile up would occur and surprisingly believe it or not as simple as the job was, pile ups often occurred.

I remember this day well because I was really tired and I had to strain my eyes to keep them open, when all of a sudden I saw something move in the peripheral vision of my eye. At first I thought my eyes were playing tricks on me when I thought I saw the ring legs that were part of the arch that held up the fragile roof was slowly sinking into the ground, so after rubbing my eyes a few times to make sure they weren't, I then noticed that dust was dropping rapidly from the roof like water, which every miner instinctively knows is a bad sign, because it meant the whole strata above was moving. Then on looking down this cross gate I could see that there were some men working near some air doors, but when the rings of this cross gate they were in began to creak and sink some more into the floor, I noticed the lights of these men were now coming towards me at rapid pace from out of this falling dust, and when they got near I heard them shouting "Run, run", and as they did it was very noticeable that the cross gate was closing in behind them. No sooner had they reached to where I had already got to safety, there was a sudden ground shaking rumble followed by a massive gush of expelled air as the main gate end of the cross gate completely collapsed. It was a complete black out, the air became so thick with dust it was really hard to breath, our cap lamps couldn't penetrate it at all, I couldn't see my hand in front of my face,and my mouth became so clogged with dust I was coughing and spitting out mud trying to keep my airway clear.

We had just lost about the link road between the two gates, which really messed the travel and supply routes up, making it twice as difficult for us to supply the face men for a while. Eventually an alternative way around it this fall was found, but the trouble was that the strata on this district was fragile and fell quite often, which meant they used more timber to shore roof falls up on the Warren house 21's district than the rest of the mine put together, so it became really hard work for us to keep them in supply.

(I have since found out from more reliable source that the main part of the collapse happened the day before and on the weekend and the incident we witnessed was the last 50 meter stretch that collapsed from the air doors only)

Face training

It was about this time I was now nearing 18 years old, so I applied to go for my full face training, but there was a waiting list and I wasn't eligible until I come of age, so it was a case of just waiting my turn. Then I heard of a mate who was doing his face training and he was only 17yr old, his dad had somehow convinced the training officer and the union that by the time he had completed his training he would be 18yr.(His dad just happened to be one of the big hitters that no one dare say anything to when he jumped the queue in the bottom). So I seized the opportunity to make that same point to both the union and training officer in question, which put them on the spot and now they couldn't argue against my request, so I got the result I wanted and within a couple of weeks I was a face trainee too (whoop whoop).

The coal face trainee was expected to learn the job of a main and a tail gate Ripper, whose job it was to drill and blast the coal and rock with explosives to tunnel forward in advance of the coal face, so the coal that is between gates could be stripped away by the coal shearing machines. The trainee also had then to learn the Waste man's job, which was to activate the hydraulic rams on all the chocks that held the up the roof and advanced the panzer conveyor for the next strip of coal, which then in banks of 12 roof supports would be individually pulled forward by the use of their hydraulic rams. The void that was left behind where coal had been extracted was then just allowed to drop the full 250 yards they had just mined (This area of no man's land was colloquially known as the Gob, and this is the reason why many houses in mining areas suffer subsidence).

At each end of the face the gate side had to be supported by wooden chocks to shore up the sides to stop the Gob collapse affecting the road ways to the face, and this was called a Pack hole which was a job that had to be learned too. More technical skills to master were such things as driving coal cutting machines, because in some cases on advance faces they could have 3 shearing machines.

At first I was sent back onto the Birkwood seam where I was already familiar with the teams there, but now onto the brand new E2 district where I hadn't worked before to learn the Main gate ripping system, which was to last for the next 20 days. In this particular gate they had a brand new Dosco tunnelling machine (The Dosco looked like a military tank but instead of a gun barrel it had a rotating cutting head on the end, and like all underground equipment it was painted brilliant white) and it was the first time a machine like this was used at our colliery to advance a coal face gate system, so it was something of a novelty at the time.

The guys I was sent with were a decent bunch and they showed me how to do things properly right from the start, and there was definitely no mucking about either, especially when I had to learn how to carry heavy steel arches on my young bony shoulders for the first time. The crown of the rings were so heavy that it took two men to carry one, but it took another man to help throw each end up onto the men's shoulders that was to carrying them, one at each end. Once loaded up we then we had to walk over obstacles and rails for about 30 meters or so, and by the time we threw this heavy steel crown arch off where it was needed, the steel had chafed the skin from my shoulder and it was bleeding. This was hard work and it took some getting used to at first, and I can definitely remember thinking I'm gonna have to beef misen up a bit!

Because I was now face training it also meant I now had to do three shifts system, and the first time on nights with this team I was asked to a work on a transfer point instead of doing face training because the district was short of men, which was acceptable as long as the deputy was prepared to book in a training shift in, otherwise I would refuse. Most deputies did without argument, but some were sticklers for the rule and they wouldn't want to do that, so me being a headstrong person I just dug my heels in until they did.

On one of these particular night shifts I was asked to operate the gate end button for the conveyor that took the coal directly from the coal face, and I didn't mind so much because I was particularly knackered that night, I was as tired as two diesel fitters put together as we used to say (This was bit of a standing joke at Sharlston, as it was often commented upon that sometimes on passing the in-bye diesel garage you could hear their alarm clocks going off!) so it was a better option to grafting all night anyway, so I was quite happy to sit there at the end of the gate and have a cushy shift, just watching the coal flow by. But that was the trouble! In just having to watch coal flow by combined with this constantly loud drone the gate end conveyor motor made, it must have hypnotised me or sung me to sleep, because the next thing I knew was when I found myself buried up to my chest in coal!

A big lump of rock or coal had got stuck in the chute and all the coal had backed up, there was so much spillage it was nearly blocking the entire roadway up and the air flow off. There must have been 40 tonne in all, I could have died there on the spot, only I had no other choice but to just get stuck in to this great pile with a shovel to try and unblock the chute as quickly as possible. I began shovelling like a mad man, desperately and frantically trying to get the conveyor going again, and all I could hear was the sound of screaming voices the face team coming over the tannoy system from in-bye, each demanding to know what the stoppage was? As soon as the chute was clear I set the conveyor rolling again, but then I had to start shovelling this massive up to the roof mountain of coal.

Luckily I managed to get it all clear by the end of the shift, but it was probably one the hardest day's work I've ever done. By the time the face team eventually arrived at the end of the gate it was all too obvious for everyone to see the massive black patch where all the wet spillage had been, and there was no hiding what had happened, but when the men saw how much I had to shovel away, they all started laughing and making comments like "did tha fall asleep old cock" and "az tha dun a bit of shovelling old lad", but all seeing the funny side of it as well. (This has happened to lots of people, not just me haha!)

For my next stint of face training I was sent down into the Barnsley seam on the SW1s district to learn the waste management system on that coal face, but little did I know at the time how infamous this district was to become to me in near future. So there I was yet again the new fresh face amongst another bunch of unfamiliar faces and still having a title as trainee, which meant I would have to suffer the usual obligatory pranks and wind ups of the men all over again, as each would play their party piece little joke on the new recruit (The prank of getting the trainee to see if he can raise a bag of cement or stone dust above his head, while someone slits the bag with a Stanley knife from behind springs to mind here, which must have been a trick that as continued for generations. My brother was once cheeky to his senior instructors in the fitting department, so they held him down and laid his long hair over the rail tracks underground, and then they cut it with a hammer). Luckily for me I had seen all these tricks and wind ups before, so I didn't fall for them, but it was all fun none the less and I can always remember laughing and smiling a lot in those days.

The SW1s coal face was a long hike, each gate was about 3000 metres long at the time, and whereas the main gate had plenty of head room, the tailgate was low and there was a steep drift to climb beforehand and after this ordeal we would then have to walk most of the journey half stooped over for quite a while before getting to the coal face. This was because the weight of the roof had virtually squashed the roof supports downwardly, which would force the floor to blow upwardly, making the gate very low and it didn't get any better until about 200 metres from the coal face, where the roof supports were quite recent and where it was possible to

Typical low gate. ©NCMME

The Runaway train

On this particular morning which was towards the end of my coal face training, I was redeployed from my tail gate ripper stint to Dinting and back Ripping the tail gate instead, with a new work buddy called Billy the Bear (Dinting was digging up the floor that had blown upwardly and back ripping was taking out the old bent roof supports and picking away the rock to re-establishing the proper roof form) this was because the tail gate was closing up and it was essential that this work was carried out. Doing this job was the same kind of work a Ripper did, and besides the deputy was booking me training shifts in, so it was fine with me.

However we were late getting onto the district due to shaft riding problems at the Sharlston end, and because of this we were told by the underground officials to climb aboard the Mine Ranger to get a ride up this long roadway to the coal face instead of the usual trudge, but mainly to make up for lost time. (A Mine Ranger was a low profile diesel locomotive that was locked on to the tracks it ran on with the use of extra sideways wheels). So we were all very pleased when we got official permission to climb aboard, but it was already loaded with some machinery called a Wooltec base pan (This was used to support the conveyor loading stage that was intended for main gate to replace one that was worn out there) so we all just got on and sat where we could, and the part of the train that I sat was on held this Wooltec pan.

When the Mine Ranger set off in-bye with us all aboard, it firstly had to climb this tail gate drift which was about 100 metres long, and it was a trip this Mine Ranger must have easily made at least a thousand times before, but for some reason this day the Mine Ranger seemed to be struggling with the weight of all the machinery and all of us onboard, even though the driver had the throttle on full revs, the diesel engine was still struggling to climb the drift, until it eventually slowed down to only a snail's pace and barely going 1 mile an hour. By this time the air was now thick with black smoke bellowing from out of the mine ranger exhaust and it was making it really difficult to see and breath, everyone on board was either coughing or having to cover their mouths up with anything they had to hand. Just as we were nearing the top of the drift it nearly came to a halt, and I can remember myself and practically everyone else onboard were virtually urging it on with our bums, (as you do) but then just as we all thought the diesel Mine Ranger was just going to make it, something suddenly went "Bang" and then "Whooosh", and no sooner it did the Mine Ranger then suddenly jolted backwards and set off at a great speed and out of control towards the bottom of the drift, where there was a raised 90 degree bend that cambered to the right. Those that could dove off straight away, some left it a bit late and ended up rolling in the dust, unfortunately both me and my work mate Billy couldn't get off, he couldn't because he was too old to react, and I couldn't because I had got my foot caught in the equipment I was riding on, and as we sped downwardly all those who managed to get off were now much further up the drift and screaming for us to jump off. I've never been so scared in all my whole life, it felt as though we were going 60 mph toward this bend, where I was certain the Mine Ranger would flip over, taking the track with it and we would surely die.

When the train hit the bend the Mine Ranger engine whipped around the corner and it managed to hold to the tracks, but when it came the turn of the last car that I was riding on it whiplashed it as it took the bend, causing my carriage to break free and take the entire train with it, which then turned onto its side, before smashing into the girders and ring legs of the adjacent roof supports. All I can remember was a massive crashing sound made by the carriages as they concertinaed towards me, and then everything flipping upside down. I also remember seeing the sparks flying off each of the roof support legs as the train grazed the side of the roadway with me still being dragged along underneath.

Within a few seconds this fully laden behemoth finally came to a crunching thudding halt, and when it did I found myself laid on my back beneath the long Wooltec plate which I had been sat on (it was about 6 metres long and about 2 metres wide with two parallel panels that were made of half inch thick steel, forming an alcove for the conveyor to go between) which had fortunately got wedged solid into the upright roof support girders making a bridge over me, or otherwise I would have been definitely crushed to death.

The first thing I noticed was that my leg was out of line from my knee, and one of my thick rubber knee pads I was wearing was shredded and cut in half! I had also lost my helmet and my lamp cable was snapped and I had even lost one of my boots. Although I was aware I had sustained some injuries, I was just so grateful to have actually survived the crash and still be in one piece, but even before I could contemplate what my injuries were, the concern for my own safety was over shadowed when I heard desperate cries of help coming from my head direction that was pointing out-bye, which was coming from my workmate Billy the Bear who like me was also laying in this wreck somewhere, but he sounded like he was in a lot more pain than me.

Within a only few moments of the crash the wreckage was surrounded by lots of lights and commotion and I could hear frantic shouting coming from the other men who had hurried down the drift to our aid. As soon as I heard them I shouted out to let them know where I was, and the first voice I heard was from that of my good mate Pete (Wacker) when I heard him shout "THERE'S ONE UNDER HERE". In only seconds after being spotted I was surrounded by my fellow workmates who immediately began lifting out of the wreck and administering me first aid. I was then placed on a stretcher where I could see the other injured bloke Billy the Bear, was also on a stretcher and he looked to be in a lot of pain. I distinctly remember going into shock on seeing my leg out of shape, but it wasn't anything compared to the immense pain in my back that was to follow. My legs were then strapped together and we were then both carried out of the mine like royalty. Which made me very proud of my fellow miners, even though I knew that most were more than happy just to be able to get out the pit early and still receive a full day's pay, but to be honest they would have done it even if their wages were docked, because this was what the comradeship down the pit was like!

As a young lad I had often played Duffs, which was a game of dare and taking chances that we used to play to see who was a chicken! But also to see who was the bravest and who would become the Duff King! This was very hazardous and not for the faint hearted, as we would often climb great heights, jump wide spaces and drop from the top of buildings to prove who was best. We only stopped doing this when one of the lads we all knew fell through a factory roof and broke nearly every bone in his body. Also to be taken into consideration was the fact I had been on all the scary rides at fun fairs at the Blackpool pleasure beach so many times I grew weary of them. I was quite fearless at that age, but that ride on the runaway Mine Ranger that day topped everything I had ever experienced, it was a wonder my hair hadn't turned white!

The underground accident even got a mention on the local TV news, and the cheeky news presenter was happy to round up the piece by making the pun "There were only minor injuries".

There was lots of concern from the area management because it looked bad for the health and safety department that a trainee had been in an accident, and they wanted to play it down. But the problem with that was this accident was the first of its kind, and it caused a full investigation into the matter because the braking system shouldn't have failed, and it was only after an inquiry had taken place, it was found that there was a flaw in the braking system. From that day on everyone around the world that was still using this type of braking system had to modify it for safety. So I guess you could say our accident achieved something at least?

When me and Billy the Bear arrived at the hospital the staff untied my legs and when they did my leg was straight again and it must have gone back in place, but there was a big hole in my knee where flesh was missing and because of this it couldn't be stitched up, but only patched over. Although I complained about my back the doctor in charge asked me to do some movements and after I did he was satisfied I was ok?

It seemed to me at the time that they were rushing me out of the hospital, they even said I didn't need an x-ray? And because l was only young I trusted the doctors and I didn't challenge this at all.

Billy Bear had broken his leg and it was in a bad way, so he was admitted to hospital, whereas I was immediately taken home by ambulance within only a few hours of the accident, and believe it or not I was still black as the ace of spades with dust, except for one leg that was spotlessly cleaned by the hospital staff, which was now covered with a great big bandage that went from my ankle up to my groin.

(Now doesn't this situation strike the reader that something very odd was going on here?) On arriving home my Mum was completely taken by surprise, she was more shocked than me that I hadn't received more care, especially after she had to wash me in front of the fire place with one cleaned leg resting on a chair, just like I was a little kid again.

The funny thing was though, as I was being washed down by my Mum, a knock came at the doo, and it was one of the other face team members who happened to be a near neighbour and he had come bearing the bad news to my Mum that I had been involved in a accident at the mine. My Mum just laughed at him and said, "I know he's here", and this guy was also shocked that I had been sent me home so quickly. It turned out that all the men assigned as stretcher bearers who were expecting to be getting an early bath on a full day's pay, were all actually sent back to the accident site to help clear all the mess up instead. (Little did I know at the time that this man bearing the belated bad news to my Mum, was to call at my house again at later date in the future, but this time bearing a different type of news).

That night in bed I was in absolute agony, not only did my knee ache really bad, but the pain in my lower back was even worse, it was so painful I must have eaten every pain killer in the house regardless of the damage it could have done to my kidneys, and still I didn't sleep a wink at all, it was like this for days on end. I was off work for 6 weeks in total, which should have been much longer, but because the incompetent doctor hadn't spotted my back injury they had only given sick notes for the minor injuries they could see, therefore pressure was put upon me to return to work by the colliery management who thought I should have been fit for work by now according to the injuries they thought I had. They also mentioned they were keen for me to complete my face training. So the upshot of it all was that I went back to work too soon as far as my health was concerned! The Bear was off work a long time and I never saw him at Sharlston again after that, I think he finished work on ill health grounds in the end!

By the time I returned back to work to finally complete my 140 days face training, the SW1s district had already finished production, and the next parallel coal face to that was the SW2s district. But I was sent back to the Warren house 21s seam to finish off my training there (it was more than likely that the training staff sent me to a different coal seam to avoid any mental trauma). On completion of my face training I was now competent in all the skills needed to work on a coal face, and now I was looking for a regular job with a team, but there were no places open, regular jobs with a face team were as rare as rocking horse shit.

This was because there was always someone waiting to fill in a slot when someone had either retired or got injured and in some cases had died. Sometimes there was a bit of nepotism as well, when places on the coal face were saved for certain members of a family, so until an opening came up I was put on the market like everyone else who didn't have a regular job (The market is a term for a spare man that could fill in anywhere when the face team was either short of men through absence or just in need of more help) which I preferred because I didn't want to get stuck in one particular job at first and doing different jobs made a change.

There was this one day I can remember working on the market all too well. I had already arrived in the Birkwood seam where I told I was to work on the coal face, but for some reason on arrival there I was then informed by the district deputy to make my way down to the new South West 2s district in the Barnsley seam and report to the Overman there in the main gate (The SW2s district was the follow on coal face that ran parallel with now infamous SW1s) So this day I set off walking down a drift to the Barnsley seam, and although I knew where this area was well, I wasn't quite sure where the new main gate was, because the way I went was like going through a rabbit warren and one could easily get lost. After I walked for about 20 minutes and passed the massive underground coal bunker, I jumped onto the conveyor and rode it until I got to the exact junction where I was told to get off, and then I went through two lots of air doors and walked up this long road way towards where I thought was the old SW1s district, but then at this point in the journey I got lost.

Was it the first gate on the left or the second I kept asking myself, because I was on the opposite side of the belt system and I no longer had a belt line to follow and trace my bearings. At one stage I was even looking for recent tracks in the stone dust to see where all the boot prints commonly headed, but it was useless the ground was wet and there were great big puddles everywhere. (Even an Indian can't track through water) At this point I was considering walking back and retracing my steps to find someone out-bye to ask which gate it was, when I suddenly noticed this dim light in the distance that was moving about, which indicated there was someone there, so I made my way towards this light. On approach I saw that it was this old man who was knelt on his knee pads and he only had his auxiliary lamp lit and he was shovelling around a manhole in the side of the rock. So I asked him where the SW2s main gate was, he didn't look at me, he just said "next left through the doors". To which I just replied "cheers bud", and then went about my way because I was late (But it did make me wonder at the time what was this old bloke was doing scratting around this manhole in the middle of nowhere?) On arrival in the main gate the deputy wanted to know where I had been up until now, and he was a bit grumpy about it, so after I had informed him of the area I had travelled from he was then ok, but when I told him the bit about getting lost and about having to ask this old bloke the way, all the other men in the vicinity who were half listening in to our conversation, suddenly stopped talking amongst themselves when they realised what I had just said, but then that silence was followed by a few Wooo's! It turned out that there was no one working out there, and I had just spoken to a ghost?

So there I laboured on the market for a year or so doing every job on the coal face, and by this time I was hoping I could land a regular job, but one that suited me, either in development or in one of the gates working as a Ripper that would allow me to be able to stay upright all shift rather than being crouched on my knees in tiny spaces because I was 6ft 3". Although that being the case, for some reason I kept getting deployed to certain job and worryingly it became a bit too regular, even though this Deputy knew I hated it because I was easily the tallest on the district, he still kept deploying me to the Pack hole where I was expected to work in a confined space of 40 inch high, shovelling and setting timber all shift long, in the dustiest and most cramped place on a coal face! After a lengthy period of time of doing this it was beginning to feel more like a punishment than a job, and the sound of the word Pack hole attached to my name at deployment time soon became synonymous with word Bot-Pittom, and likewise I became sick of it. So once again I was urgently looking for a way out of a situation and even considering getting a transfer to another shift just to rid myself of this twisted pit deputy.

Then one day my luck changed when my mate called Pete who was the same guy that pulled me out of the train wreck, who just happened to be the Chock fitter on our coal face team, mentioned that their department was suffering a shortage of men, so I asked him to put a good word in for me, to which he agreed. No sooner had we both got out of the mine we called into the Chock fitting office to see the boss of that department. To my surprise after only a brief conversation about my knowledge of mechanics and engineering, and a few phone calls were made, he instantly informed me that I was now a Chock fitter! Then surprisingly, although I had no experience whatsoever, and only after receiving an handful of tools to hang on my belt, the Chock fitter boss asked then me if I wanted to help out by covering a district that very same afternoon, and being so grateful for the new job I felt obliged. So instead of going to get showered and going home on my Kawasaki motorbike as usual, I rejoined the queue on the Bank side and went straight back down the pit to cover a district as a Chock fitter! Even though I hadn't any training I had a good knowledge of mechanics and hydraulics wasn't rocket science to me, and it didn't take a genius to replace a broken ram pins or change the odd burst hydraulic hose, so I was confident enough to carry on for the time being and happy to leave all the technical stuff until later.

A New Start

That first shift as a Chock fitter was a piece of cake, every job I was called to I coped with well, which made me more enthusiastic about my new job and I couldn't wait for my next shift to come. The following day I was deployed from the pit top Chock fitter's office this time, and from there I was sent back on to my old district with Pete the shift Chock fitter to commence my training in hydraulics. But when I turned up on the district this twisted deputy tried to deploy me to the Pack hole again, and when me and Pete told him I wasn't on the team anymore, he nearly had a fit, his face was contorting and straining to take it in, it was an absolute picture to see and it was obvious to everyone his face was put out of joint and he wasn't happy. He was so determined to reverse the decision that allowed me to be a Chock fitter he got straight on the phone to the under manager to complain that the team were now short of men (What a twat he was!) He wasn't successful though and it wasn't long before I was fully trained up and competent in that job and was soon working on my own as a Chock fitter.

The job entailed maintaining the hydraulic roof supports that ran the length of the coal face, and depending on its length determined how many of these chocks there would be, usually it was around 250 chocks plus, and all pressurised by huge electric pumps that were fed from a 500 gallon hydraulic reservoir. The average working pressure the Chocks worked on was about 2000psi but in some cases it could as high as 3000psi, which could be very dangerous especially if a hose was to burst and someone was next to it. Each chock had a

Faceline hydraulic roof supports (Chock). ©NCMME

Face shearer cutting coal. ©NCMME

handle that rotated on a dial to select a particular movement of the chock and this was a part of the block that housed lots of valves that made the hydraulics work, it was a bit technical and the equipment required constant maintenance.

Discounting that, some face team officials took it upon themselves when they were short of men on a shift, to try and integrate the chock fitter into the face team to carry out coal face work instead, thus undermining union policy of one man one job, especially on the night shift when men didn't turn up for work, so I often found myself at loggerheads not only with staff but also with the face men as well, who thought I should pitch into help them regardless of my job title. It didn't bother them in the slightest to try and undermine my job status and get me to do two jobs, which was in fact actually undermining their own protection under the working practices that were laid down by their own union, which was only achieved through years of struggle and fighting for these rights. (My theory is that they thought that because I was face trained and I wasn't qualified as a craftsman, my job status wasn't real or a priority measured against coal production? Although I had loads of work to complete to satisfy my own boss, and report sheets to fill out of all the work I had completed at the end of each shift, my fellow workmen gave it no consideration whatsoever, and despite the fact that there would be a fitter or electrician in each of the gates who had nothing to do all shift but cover for break downs, they never got pestered and their refusal to help out was never questioned).

Job recognition

At one period in time I was asked to go with a different face team on a temporary basis, but still working on SW2s in the Barnsley seam, because their regular chock fitter was sent to a new development. The hydraulic chocks on this face were ancient and they hadn't been out of the pit for a overhaul in ten years or more, they were pure rust and they should have never been installed on a coal face, These Chocks were so rotten that the hydraulic legs that held the canopy up to the roof would sometimes push through a half inch thickness of steel, which meant the whole canopy had to be replaced. The hoses on the chock legs burst all the time, and rams constantly broke and needed replacing, and these were usually cemented in place by years of dried mud that set like concrete which made them very difficult to remove, and they usually fell to bits when getting them out. Chock legs would split wide open with the weight from the roof, not to mention the amount of Ram bolts that kept snapping all the time, and nearly every hexogen nut would round off when a spanner was applied. It was an absolute nightmare of a job which needed at least two chock fitters per shift just to get it up to a reasonable standard, and because we were undermanned the maintenance fell way behind.

Every day I was crawling the 250 yards of the coal face from one end to the other all shift long, answering to the screams of "Chock fitter wanted" coming from the face tannoy system and constantly demanding my presence. It was too much for one man and although the mechanical fitters were told by their superiors to help out, they never did. It was a soul destroying and I was constantly dripping wet through with hydraulic soluble oil and sweat. In one shift I held the record for changing 4 legs and 6 rams and because of this the Chock fitter boss made a rare appearance to check on all the work we had carried out. (He couldn't believe how much tackle we were using) It was futile trying to keep up with the break downs and the management knew this, they agreed that when this face was finished that all the chocks were to be left on the coal face and not to be salvaged. But in the meantime it was a case of just having to knuckle down and do my best.

To make matters worse this team of men I was sent to work with were predominantly from the Sharlston area, whereas other teams were usually made from a mix up from other towns that came there when their colliery closed. The blokes on this team took an instant dislike to me, I don't know if it was because I was a Normanton lad or maybe they just didn't like me? But I highly suspect it was because their Chock fitter before me would roll over backwards for them and give in to them if they were short of men on the night shift and fill in doing face team work instead. I also think that when they met me they thought I would do the same, but me being a one man one job type of person, and the fact that we could hardly keep up with repairs as it was, I didn't cave in and I quite rightly refused. I remember it striking me at the time that it was no wonder we couldn't keep up with the maintenance because the Chock fitter before me hardly ever handed in a work done report on his turn on the night shift, which made it abundantly clear that he spent more time doing other face workers jobs instead!

After a short while working with this team I was then informed it was to be my regular job with them from then on, because their old chock fitter was staying on this new development permanently. This is when I found out the reason why the chock fitting department was desperate for men in the first place, it was because they needed replacements for this new super face that needed getting ready urgently, and this was called Warren House 44s district, which had brand new gear with the latest hydraulic chocks on a bigger seam of coal where men could actually stand up on the coal face.(That was the big idea, but it ended up a living nightmare) The Chocks were massive compared to what we had seen before, and although they were hydraulic they were controlled by electricity, which meant all the cream of the Chock fitter department had to have an upgrade in their training. So all the best chock fitters ended up on the new Warren House 44s, which required two Chock fitters per shift until it got underway, even though everything was brand new?. All the while there was me left to struggle all on my own day after day and getting no help from anyone and it was impossible to keep up with the work, but what made it more unbearable was the hostile relationship that developed between me and this team which gradually began to wear me down, and on top of that, because I was always wet through with emulsifying oil and I had to climb inside hydraulic tanks to clean them out, the fumes must have affected my chest because I developed a serious case of bronchitis (The smoking and dust didn't help either).

So it wasn't long before I started having time off work with a bad chest, and as a result I was eventually called in to see the personnel manager, who was new at Sharlston because Claude had since retired, to explain my absences from work, but my sick notes to hand and excuses fell on deaf ears, this personnel manager even made the argument that I shouldn't even be working down the mine if I had bronchitis (How did he think I had got it in the first place? The pit was a Petri dish of diseases that spread around the mine with the air flow, especially in the winter time, men constantly played ping pong with the same flu and infections, sometimes getting the same flu three times over). None the less I got an attendance warning despite not being in nice place as far as my health was concerned, and looking back at the situation, I think this warning was instigated from someone else?

It wasn't long after this warning I was working on the day shift and I was urgently requested in the tailgate, because the tail gate hydraulic Ramming station that was supposed to ram the face conveyor to the coal when advancing the gate, had completely fallen to bits and it needed rebuilding straight away. Bolts had sheared and fittings had snapped off, hoses had broken off rams, and hydraulic fluid was squirting everywhere, turning all the ground spillage underfoot into this thick mud that was half way up my shins, which constantly tried to suck my boots off every time I moved. It was a right mess and all of this mud that stunk of hydraulic emulsifying oil had to be cleared away firstly before I could even locate where the hoses were burst, never mind begin rebuilding it.

The atmosphere was frantic, everyone was panicking because the face conveyor pans needed to be advanced forward at least twice before the coal face shearer could continue cutting. This was because the ramming station had collapsed on the previous night shift, which meant that gate was now two cuts behind in advancement. I was specifically told to stay there and do anything I could to get it working by both the Chock fitting dept and the tail gate deputy! But all the shift long all I could hear on the coal face tannoys was the desperate screams of the face team shouting "Chock fitter wanted" as one hose after another burst and ram pin broke on the coal face, and the screams got more nasty and insulting by the hour, but I could do nothing about that, I had strict instructions to stay put to assist, so the shearer could cut in and out of the gate at least twice before it could head back to the main gate.

By the time the end of the shift came I was totally exhausted and again dripping wet through with sweat and hydraulic oil, all I wanted to do was just go home. No sooner had I reached Lifting station where I could finally have a sit down and have a breather while the Man rider train arrived, I was approached by a senior union man who was a member of our face team, and he had some other team members by his side for support, who instead of him taking me to one side and talking to me in private and in a more appropriate manner, he took it upon himself to start questioning me in front of everyone there as to where I had been all the shift, and asking why I didn't attend their calls when I was shouted. Regardless of being informed of what I was actually doing all shift by the tailgate official who just happened to be present, he and the others had their minds up that the real reason was that I had been slacking it off! And this union man then announced that he was going to get me moved to another team? Even though the tail gate team backed me up! He wasn't listening and he had already made his mind up to get rid of me. So in realising his attitude wasn't going to change, I gave up arguing my case and took the alternative stance of deliberately winding him up instead by sarcastically making the comment, "I've been sat on my arse all shift tossing it off", also adding, "Why, what are you going to do about it anyway!" Which obviously wasn't true, but I purposely goaded him because he was supposed to be my union man and his job was to represent me as well, and he had no right to address me that way in front of everyone else, besides that I wanted to make sure he kept his promise to get me moved to another shift or coal face, because I dreaded the thought of having to stay with this team any longer (My brother had warned me beforehand about the attitude of a few of the Sharlston men, which he had discovered after he was transferred there when the St John's Colliery had closed, he said that they were a bit too clicky (cliquey) and hard to get along with, adding, that they all had certain ways that were peculiar to us Normanton folk. So armed with this knowledge it became my summation at the time, that because they were the original workforce there they perhaps wanted to keep control of the politics of the colliery?

(I added this particular tale not to moan about it, or give it the "poor old me", but to make a point regarding the union's attitude, which will become much clearer later on in this story)

When the following Monday morning arrived, I walked into the Chock shop on the surface to get my duties for the day from my boss as usual, and guess what? I was immediately informed by my boss that I was to be moved on to another face team, but he also went on to explain that he had heard the point of view that came with the request to move me, but he didn't buy their argument for one second, he knew I was a top worker on his squad, and he also informed me that not only did this union mans interference instigate me getting moved to another the team, but it also instigated an enquiry by the mechanical engineer's department, who after investigating the original complaint about the status of Chock fitters doing face work, he ordered that from that day on all Chock fitting staff were restricted to doing Chock fitting work only (It wasn't long afterwards that because of the technology in that field of hydraulics became more advanced, as a consequence the Chock fitters of the day needed more training, which eventually made it a skilled job). As a result the working status of a Chock fitter at Sharlston was never questioned again from that day on. The icing on the cake for me was that the new team I was sent with was full of all my mates who I attended the Leeds United games with at Elland road and sometimes boozed with on weekends. So on hearing this great news it felt like a massive weight had been lifted off me and things were now beginning to brighten up again. (It felt just like that bit in the film *Wizard of Oz*, when the picture goes from black and white and changes into Technicolor).

A New Beginning

At last I got to work with my mates and a younger set of lads who had similar senses of humour, and now we could at least have a laugh together, which everyone knows makes the shifts pass quicker. It seemed at the time that this team I was sent with had its fair share of the popular characters of our generation at Sharlston, and nearly all of them were on the same level of acting daft as me, so from then on I started to enjoy going to work again, even though I was still constantly hailed from one end of the coal face to the other and kept very busy, it was now more bearable because unlike the other shift, these guys understood that these old chocks were knackered and that I had a lot on my plate, and lots of times they would even offer to help out !

Each generation of the men at the mine had their own heroes and big hitters and characters, and I guess my generation was the next supply of young men that would also makes names for themselves in the future, either through leadership, hard work, or through other popular activities outside the industry. We had a few stars of the Rugby league circuit, Boxers, Footballers, Cricketers, there were many others with all sorts of skills. There were some that were even famously known for just for how much beer they could drink or how notoriously strong or tough they were. There were also what we called the big money men who also were admired by many, these were a usual collection of the same faces that would practically live underground, grabbing every bit of overtime there was, working double shifts both week days and weekends.

Some did it because they had big families, others did because they liked to spend as much time as they could going on holidays abroad, and these types were easily recognisable by the permanent golden brown tans they adorned all year round. There were also those who just wanted nice things! It wasn't unaccustomed for us on arrival at the coal face gate ends to find men sprawled out and throwing out zzzzz's, catching up on sleep who hadn't been home from the day before, and it was always the same usual faces.

There was this one guy called Tilly, who looked more like the character Jason King than Jason King did, and he was one of the permanent tan brigade, and all the younger generation thought he was ace, because he was loads of fun and he never stopped smiling which helped to brighten up the atmosphere of what was normally a dull one. Another one of these regular overtime monsters had a large family, so he practically had to live down the mine to support them, and he was nicknamed Honey, because he called everyone else Honey, and he was so tight fisted that if he ever cadged a pinch of snuff from someone they might not get the snuff tin back, he was notorious for always trying to pocket it, and he was a tough bloke who had a strong jaw line and a high cheek bone structure that reminded me of a Hyena, and by all accounts when he was young man no one would dare have him a fight, and because of his past reputation, when on the occasions he cadged a bit of snuff, perhaps some were too frightened to ask for it back. (I personally know this because he tried it on with me, but I had the resolve of Bugs Bunny and there was no way he was going to knick my snuff. At first he denied having it, but I stood over him with hand out and kept repeating "give me my snuff" until I got it back) There was another one of these overtime grabbers who was an unusual exception to the rest, and he was called Clint, who just happened to be the same lad that got to do his face training at 17 yr old. He worked every hour God as sent from a young lad, and to this day he is still grafting in the mines in just about every country in the world, and apparently he is in big demand.

The Three Shift System Syndrome

I had a few years of this overtime grabbing, working all hours just to make ends meet, and working double and sometimes treble shifts, but after a while of working like this on top of the three shift system, it eventually wears you down and you can become a bit confused.

After coming home one morning from a night shift I was so tired that when I got in bed I slept through the next day and right past my next shift on nights. When I did eventually get up and go to work, I couldn't understand why we had jumped a day; I thought all my mates were playing a practical joke on me until they showed me the newspaper with the days date on it. (Another thing that was peculiar was the fact that none of my family even noticed I was still in bed?) There was another time when I was on the day shift, when I happened to wake up and on taking a tired glance at the alarm clock I must have misread the time, and convinced myself I had over slept. After quickly jumping out of bed I dashed out of the house and set off in the car to pick up my mate Vic, who I expected would be waiting for his lift to work. But when I got to his house it was in darkness, so I had to knock him up out of bed, and when he came to the window he was still half asleep, which made him easier to convince him that like me we had over slept, to which he didn't waste any time getting dressed and rushing out to the car. We then drove off at a racing speed to try to get the pit on time, but on arrival the pit canteen was all in darkness and there wasn't a soul in sight, which was really confusing at first, until we both entered the pit baths to look at the clock in the time office... it was only

4.30 am. My mate Vic was normally known to be laid back and an easy going sort of bloke, but he really liked his sleep, so he wasn't very happy about what I had done, all he kept saying was "I can't believe it, thaz lost me all that sleep ya twat", over and over again. It took him ages to forgive me (but we laugh about it now).

Another confusing time was long before I could afford any transport of my own. I was waiting in a shop doorway on the housing estate for the pit bus just like many did, and this particular morning it was raining really heavy and a car pulled up, and the driver who was a deputy at the pit called Colin wound his window down and shouted for the first three men over to give them a lift, which was a usual thing that some car owners did. So the first three men stepped over which included myself, and the first guy to the car opened the front passenger side door and tried to pull the front seat forward to let the other passengers into the back seats, but he couldn't do it and he seemed to be struggling. All the while me and this other bloke were getting wet through by the rain, I was even having to hold a newspaper over my head, eventually the driver got out of the car to try to move the seat forward, but just like the first man he was struggling with it too, and now he was getting really wet as well, until I looked at the car and noticed it had four doors, so I just opened the rear door and got in, and on doing so Colin said, "fucking hell what am I doing here?" It turned out he had just exchanged his old two door for a four door, and the first guy that approached his car was his regular pick up, and was used to the old car as well, which just happened to be the same make and colour!

Later when I was getting changed in the pith bath lockers I couldn't wait to tell everyone about it, and there I was telling the tale and making everyone laugh about how ridiculous the situation was, when I heard Colin's voice shout from the next bay of lockers "dun't worry thy wain't be gerrin a lift no more, am tellin thee naa", and do you know what? He never offered me a lift again from that day on!

There were lots of character types at Sharlston of every shape height and width. There was this huge giant of man called Les who was a main gate Ripper, who happened to be an ex rugby star and he could pick up pieces of steel that two men would struggle with like it was nothing to him, and he was a gentle giant who was well respected! There was also this guy that we often joked was the fattest bloke in the world called Johnny, who was often the centre of some form of controversy in the showers that always ended with the use of hose pipe to blast him down as far as I can remember?

On the opposite end of the scale to him was a really small guy who was about four foot six and his face and hair resembled one of those rubber Gonk dolls that children bought to put on the end of their pencils. His eyebrows made Dennis Healey's brows look tidy and he also had webbed fingers too, and on top of that he had what we called Doney-Wakey eyes (one staring at Wakefield and the other staring oppositely towards Doncaster) not only that he could barely talk and was only capable of doing the simplest of jobs. We called him Kid because he called everyone else Kid and he was a nice old guy and everyone liked him, some even went to the lengths of protecting him from any of the usual ridicule or piss take. Thinking about it some of those older men that were recruited many years beforehand would have never passed the medical of my day, which just showed how much the industry had changed over a period of time, compared to how hard it was to get a job at the pit in 1975!

There were people from different nations and different backgrounds and in all the time I was there this was never an issue, we were all miners together, yes we took the piss sometimes but it was always in good humour that was equally reciprocated, but that was in the days before people started to become offended by everything!

One foreign national in particular was from Iraq and he came to work at Sharlston at the height of the Iran-Iraq war, I think he was getting away from that. None the less he was a nice lad and a good worker and he got on with everybody.

After a while of getting to know him, we once accidentally bumped into each other in popular pub in Wakefield called the Spaniard. He had his parents in his company and they had come over to the UK to visit their son, noticing this and me being an inquisitive type of person I naturally found myself drawn towards his parents, and it wasn't long before me and my missus were sat down and chatting away with them, and although his father only had small command of the English language his son was quite happy to interpret for us to bridge the gaps. And I wanted to know everything, so as one can imagine we talked plenty, all about the war, the oil crisis and reserves, their lifestyle, all sorts of things, and obviously the more we talked the more I had to drink!

I think his Dad told me he was big in construction in Baghdad and he was in charge of building waterways and digging drainage systems and other similar projects. It was in this conversation we somehow got talking about work opportunities in Iraq, and because I think he had taken a liking to me he offered me a job. I can't exactly remember the precise details of the role I was to play, but it think it was something like the position of a foreman, and on enquiring about what the wages would be like, his son assured me my lifestyle would be far superior to here in Britain. It was at this point I definitely recall raising my concerns about the ongoing war in there, and about the fighter jets and rockets coming from Iran, but after his Dad assured me that the air defence systems that encircled Baghdad were impenetrable, it was only then that I agreed to go. On hearing this, his Dad stood to his feet and gave me a big hug followed by his customary handshake and then we all sat down. Leaving me now quite happily discussing the finer details of how we were going to manage it with my wife Deb. Though all the while I was talking to my wife, his son was staring at me with a look of concern on his face, so I asked him what was a matter, to which he replied "you do realise my Dad means it, he is dead serious". I don't know what I said but I must have impressed upon him I was serious too!

None the less a couple of weeks went by before I saw this lad again because we were on different shifts and our paths hardly crossed, but when I did he told me his Dad had expressed his deep disappointment at me for not being at the airport on the date that we had agreed. On hearing this news it made me feel really guilty and because it had completely escaped my mind for the obvious beer reasons, and also the fact it was the first time ever that I had let someone down like that, I asked my mate if there was any way to make it up to his Dad or would he accept my apologies, to which my Iraqi mate just laughed and said "awww forget it, I've already explained to my Dad that you're British and he shouldn't have taken you serious after you had drunk all that beer".

(I lied, I let Captain Neat down as well, I didn't turn up to take my part 1 in the Army Cadets, I forgot about that one, Soz Captain Neat)

We had a Jehovah's Witness on one of the coal faces and the first time I met him I thought "what a very nice chap he was", I had never met anyone so polite before. It wasn't long before we both got chatting away in the gate, but all the while I couldn't help noticing sniggers coming from the other lads, so on noticing this and no sooner I took a break from talking to this Jehovah's Witness, I couldn't wait to ask the others what the big joke was, and they couldn't wait to tell me either. They bet me that he would soon get on about God and afterwards he would be giving me a booklet to read. So I just laughed and thought "Whatever!" By the end of the shift I knew all about Jehovah and gained a little booklet too! The lads were proper buggers though, they would keep teasing him to make him swear and break his vows, and no matter how much he resisted temptation they got to him in the end, as a consequence he completely flipped his lid and began chasing all the blasphemers that had taunted him with a seven pound lump hammer, determined to punish some God back into them!

There was this Polish bloke who used to live a couple of streets away from me and no matter how severe the weather conditions were he would always ride to work on his green Honda 200, and sometimes I would pass his house on a icy cold winter's morning making my way over the fields to work, wearing two coats on and hat and gloves because it was so bitter, and I would see this guy ride past me with his crash helmet barely sat on his head with his chin strap loose because it was too small, and only wearing an Hawaiian shirt that was unbuttoned and a string vest underneath.

There was one bloke who everyone used to see making his way from the Colliery after he had finished his shift, and although we had pit showers he wouldn't use them and he went home as black as the fire back every day!

Each generation would have their share of characters who were the in crowd of their day, and equally so would contain their fair share of men who were far too intelligent to be working in a coal mine, who had either lost their way or got held back like my Dad, or they were just satisfied with what they had at hand and were happy just having a simple life. Although each generation seemed to be miles apart in the way they thought, common sense always prevailed between the ages.

End of an Era

SW2s lasted for three and half years and followed the seam of coal for over 4000 metres before it came to the end of its life, and in that time even though I had a shaky start, I had some of the best times and funniest moments in my whole mining career, because we were fortunate to have good officials and team members, each with their own particular peculiarities and eccentricities, but we also had the odd ones who were just plain stupid. For instance: One day the shearer had leaked so much oil from its hydraulics it could no longer operate, and there wasn't a proper mobile oil container on the district, nothing smaller than a 45 gallon drum that would fit on the coal face, so this guy trying to impress everyone to how committed he was to the production of coal, emptied out his full bottle of drinking water that was to last him the whole shift and he used it to transported the much needed oil to the machine? Now that's stupid!

The rest of the lads were just crazy and made up from just about every nut from every town in the vicinity, who would do anything for a laugh, and much to the annoyance of our Overman we had nicknamed Peffer, who often jokingly said to me "it wasn't too bad until I came along". He was a good bloke and he laughed with us most of the times, but sometimes he would blow his top and go in to tirades about splitting the team up, but he liked them all really. On one occasion we were all walking in-bye between the gate ends at the start of a shift, and this cross gate went up and down with hidden dips that were called swilly's, and these were usually full of black rancid water that stunk! This water was an accumulation of mine water, human urine, mice urine, oil and a lot of other undesirable things that would make you poorly, we even joked that there was a creature living in it just like the one in the *Star Wars* film dumpster scene where a snake thing with one eye pops up out of the murky water.

This Swilly swamp was over boot top deep and the only way to get past it was to perform a tightrope style walk balancing act on one of the rail tracks that was still above the water, but if someone lost their balance and fell off, they would get their boots full of this toxic black foot rotting liquid for the rest of the shift, so it was vital to have good balance, but hardly a day went by without some poor sod getting the black foot of death! The funny thing was that when someone did fall in everyone would start imitating the circus big top medley, pipe organs and all. The day when Peffer filled his boots we all in perfect harmony recreated the tune for his and our entertainment, but he didn't see the funny side of it, and he completely flipped his lid and went into one of his usual tirades about how stupid we all were and he didn't spare my name when it came to apportioning the blame as the culprit of all the silliness.

The truth of the matter was that we took our work seriously and wanted to achieve as much as we could to earn more money, and all this acting daft was just our way of dealing with the crappy environment we had to work in day in day out. Nevertheless it was much to the irritation of the older officials who were set in their ways; they couldn't understand our generation's sense of humour (A generational thing). I think the thing that most irritated them was the use of a odd list of musical instruments that were either manufactured there on site, or brought from home, which we would use to make unusually daft noises over the tannoy system that no one expected to hear down the mine. The list of these offending items was: hydraulic hoses which we used as trumpets, a Jews harp, a Duck caller, a Cuckoo's caller, and just about anything else we could use to make a strange sound.

It was tolerated for a while, until one day the surface control informed us that the General Manager had been listening in on our Tom Foolery and he said he was thinking about having a purge of the team and splitting us all up, so we had to stop these shenanigans for a spell. In the mean time as a more subdued continuation of this type of fun, a particular hydraulic chock was chosen by you know who? That was half way along the coal face and it was painted up with different coloured luminous paints and decorated with the sort of items that were normally seen on front of an old dust cart lorry, like little dolls and other similar things, it was also covered in the scribbles of prophetic wisdoms penned by anyone who happened to crawl past it and who also just happened to have a marker pen handy. In bold letters on either side of its canopy it read, I AM THE HAPPY CHOCK! It was supposed to cheer us up! Later it actually got recognised as reference place name that was used whenever someone wanted to describe where the shearer or someone was on the coal face!

On the few occasion we had breakdowns, either at the coal face or out-bye that had stopped production, in those times and if all other work was up to scratch and all the officials were busy somewhere else on the district trying to get the breakdown fixed, we would often hold the Games!

The Games consisted of anything from press ups, weight lifting, dips, and sit ups, and even seeing who could hang from steel arches the longest by their arms with added weights tied to their belts, but not without the obligatory cheating or the prank playing as well. One time we had set up two temporary bench pressing platforms made with planks across two lots of timber blocks, and using two inch wide steel dowel rods for bars we then loaded each end up with 5 gallon drums full of water to make dumbbells. At one point we had this big stocky bloke in competition with a skinny runt of a lad, both with a bench and bar with four 5 gallon drums suspended at each end, but what the bigger guy didn't realise was that although he was lifting full heavy drums, the skinny runts drums were completely empty, and the big guy couldn't understand why he was being beat, and he nearly had an heart attack trying to beat this lad, but no matter how much he tried he couldn't. It was a right laugh when he found out the reason why!

There was this one guy who got slightly injured at the start of the night shift and he had to go out the mine early to receive some medical attention, and we all joked at the time that he might catch his missus in bed with another bloke, and when he arrived home he actually did and it was his mate from the opposite shift. This didn't go down well with our team at all, and because of this incident his so called mate never returned back to the pit for some reason?

Another fun pastime we had was at the end of every shift, but only if we were travelling out-bye from the tailgate end, because tailgate like its predecessor on SW1s was extremely low all the way out, and likewise the weight on that gate was constant, which meant men were permanently placed there to back rip and replace girders that were badly bent and to dint the floor, which made it a very long hike on foot, especially half stooped over. To get around this we would take advantage of the fact the gate had a slight downhill incline towards out-bye and right to the gate end, and if a flat supply bogie was available the men would set it running and jump on board. Usually four men to one bogey that could pick up tremendous speeds at times, and the riders would have to hang on for dear life as this steel four wheeled bogey would follow the rails, going up and down dips and tilt from side to side with the camber of the track, and all the while we would be crouching as low as we could get to avoid hitting our heads on either a bent girder or even worse, getting it taken off by the sharp edge of a corrugated sheet that was forced down with the weight of the roof.

These bogeys could go so fast that if they left the rails there was a good chance it would cause a few injuries, so it was down to the Brake man at the back of the Bogey to slow it down if needed, which was done by the use a piece of timber about double the width of a fence paling that he would jam between the wheel and the frame of the tram, especially on bad bits of tracks where the bogey might come off the rails. Sometimes the piece of wood used for breaking would smoke with the amount pressure put on it, because the bogey was already heavy to start with, but when it was loaded with the added weight of the men it created more inertia going downhill, which meant it could reach speeds of up to 30mph in some places, and if that wasn't scary enough, sometimes if the brake man on the bogey in front was braking a bit too cautiously, he was more likely to get shunted by the reckless nutter who was running break free from behind. Not many people dare ride out like this, it was too dangerous for some, but it was something we did, and it wasn't for the timid or faint hearted, it was mainly a preserve of the nutcases only. Although there were a number of derailments and crashes over the years, I can't remember anyone getting hurt too seriously, but it was definitely an experience and perhaps one of the best adrenalin rushes I've ever had in all my life!

Although the underground Christmas parties were legendary throughout the whole of the British coal fields I can only describe ours which became more exorbitant by the year, and sometimes by the time the last night shift entered the gate carrying their feast, they could expect to be greeted by a mountain of goodies that were left over from the previous two shifts that were laid out on sheets of Brattish (Coated sheeting), and carefully wrapped and covered to stay fresh, so by the time the night shift added their little lot, it would have resembled a scene that would put any Arabian dessert feast to shame.

During that period of time working on South West two's, I managed to own a couple of motorbikes, passed my driving test, bought my first car, got married and was very happy to receive my first child, but the down side of that period of time was that we saw the demise of a few good men, some through injuries and ill health and some just simply passed away, and the worst thing of all was that we still had Margaret Thatcher as the Prime Minister!

It was a bleak period of time for the labour movement, the Conservative government had won much of the country over with a ploy that was in the form of giving tax concessions, which they achieved through cutting down the size of government and encouraging the selloff of state owned public assets, and because everyone's was then paying less tax, their wages seemed to grow by the year and suddenly everybody was starting to have a bit of spare cash in their pockets, and people chose to ignore the warnings from the left wing parties of how it would only be a short term fix until everything was sold off, and from then on everything we used to get for free we would then have to pay for in the future, eventually causing these things to be too expensive to afford in the end!

Despite those warnings the majority of people at that time didn't care, they had become a part of this new selfish society that had been socially condition and groomed to believe everything they saw and heard on TV. But if you also take into account that when we had a succession of labour governments in power that took nearly half our wages in taxes and people could hardly ever afford luxuries and everything was too expensive to buy, it was no surprise people were fed up and wanted the same wage comparisons of other countries like the US and in some European countries like Germany, where they seemed to have much better standards of living than us? So again it was no surprise people lost faith in the Labour party and the left.

A good example of this imbalance was made obvious to us one day when we were all stood outside the lamp room waiting to go underground on a typical hot sunny afternoon. It was when this luxury coach came into the yard, which was so modern it looked like a spaceship to us, and when it parked up outside the main offices all these really smart men got off it who were all wearing tailored suits and gold watches. We were told they were visitors from the German mining industry, so everyone automatically assumed that they were senior management or directors? Later that afternoon they all came crawling through the same coal face I was working on, and on these visitors passing where a few of us were working, I couldn't help ask them who they were and why they had come to visit us, only to be shocked to hear them say that they were just ordinary miners like us, and it turned out they were on treble the wages that we were on, and they laughed at how backward our system of mining was! We were all left gobsmacked, it was a real eye opener to us, and no sooner had these German visitors got out of earshot just about everyone began shaking their heads and virtually echoing the same sentiments of disgust, that went something like this: "Ayup, I thought it was us that won the bloody war" or "Our Government must be having a right laugh at us Mugs!"

150 WALWORTH ROAD, LONDON SE17
TEL: 01-703 0833

The Labour Party

1983

MEMBERSHIP CARD

NAME MR. Mc GOWAN

ADDRESS 8. CEDAR RD.

NORMANTON

W/YORKSHIRE

PARTY NORMANTON. C.L.P.

ORDINARY

Politics

By this time I was already a door knocking canvassing member of the Labour party and I had not only become well read in many left wing pieces of literature, but also in a few right wing pieces as well, and after I had studied both sides of the political spectrum I concluded that the only way was Socialism at that moment in time.

As the years rolled by what began as a temporary fix until I got a better job and now stretched to twelve in total, and I had continued in my trade as a Chock fitter going from one coal face to the next and following each particular seam until it was completely worked out, and by this time I was more mature and educated in many different ways.

One major thing I learnt came from another bloke called Vic who worked on the same coal face as me. He was the number two shearer driver in the tailgate end and he told me that I could even restore my lungs by using the yogi method of teachings which he had also learnt from a small green book he had bought, which he then gave to me and insisted that I read it. Only after a short while of receiving this book and studying its contents and carrying out its instructions, I found out it actually worked! My bronchitis began to clear up and my breathing got better, so from then on I started taking care of my health. I gave up smoking and started swimming, went running and even boxing in the ring, and finally I ended up being a bit of a body builder. Not only was I now gaining knowledge by lifting books but also gaining muscle and strength by lifting weights! Which gave me much more confidence and my outlook on life began to change from then on! So thanks Vic! God bless rest in peace.

It was around this time I began taking an interested in union politics, and I started attending union meetings on a Saturday mornings, because I felt a lot of issues needed to be raised, which was usually done at the end of the meeting under: Any other business! In only a short period of time I became well versed in how union matters worked at both local and national levels and this enabled me to be able to articulate what was actually going on when asked by my fellow workmates, and because I took the time to explain in depth, and in a way that was easy to understand, and also the fact that I always openly expressed my opinions as to whether decisions were made rightly or wrongly, I think over a period of time of doing this, although it was unintentional, it must have gained me a lot more respect amongst the younger generations, who were already of the opinion that they had no real representation on the union. Although I did agree that the union desperately needed new blood and I knew they would have given me support, I had no intentions of standing in the union branch elections at that present moment in time.

The reason why I had no ambition to become a politician or a union man, was that I didn't think I was informed enough to have the confidence to step into any political arena or take up the reins of a union representative or leader at that time, I was still a bit young and naive in those matters and I needed to gain a lot more knowledge and experience firstly.

Fortunately just around the corner came an opportunity when I was informed of a day release course that was available to all NUM members (National Union of Mine workers) for higher education in industrial relations and politics. On hearing this news I went straight into the union office to get a form, and I can distinctly remember hearing some disparaging sneers from a couple of the union men at the time when I was asking for it, none the less it just spurred me on even more to send it in. But there was a snag and that snag was a selection process that I had to get by first, which could have been the reason the sneers in the office were all about. There were only 14 places available and 140 candidates who all wanted to study industrial relations at Leeds University. It was a three year course that was set at diploma level which was a sponsored education programme set up by both the union and British coal to educate union officials to improve the standard of dialogue in industrial relations between the two parties.

On the day of the selection process I arrived at King Arthur's Castle in Barnsley where it was taking place to find a packed hall full of men, all seated and awaiting for the talent show to begin. Well this is how I figured it because it was obvious to me the selectors would be choosing certain types of people, and on looking around there looked to be a lot of what I thought these certain types were supposed to look like, but I certainly didn't put myself in that category.

When the selection process began we were all instructed to listen to a following lecture, and all the while we were all to take down notes, afterwards transcribe those notes in an understanding of what we had just heard, the senior lecturer then stated that those notes we had made were also needed for examination. After that there was a questions and answers paper, followed by a succession of debates, where we had all been split into separate groups. It was at this point I finally got to use my best asset, which was my big mouth and boy oh boy did I use it to its fullest capacity, in doing so I practically dominated every debate that took place that morning, and to my surprise they must have been looking for the big mouthy type, because I managed to win a place at the Leeds University.

So from then on every Wednesday instead of crawling up and down a coal face and being constantly hailed from one end to the other, I was now afforded the luxury of being able to start at 9 am in the morning, and was able to wear some smart clothes for a change and sit in the sophisticated surroundings of the adult education centre (which was in the very oldest part of the university and it was a beautiful building) just taking it easy relaxing in a big old leather high backed chair alongside all my new student buddies, sat around a big oak table with a constant flow of coffee, tea and biscuits! On the syllabus for each day there would be English which included grammar, speech writing, oration and media awareness, history of the Labour movement, Politics, Economics and theories, and all aspects of Law, criminal, civic industrial etc, and there to give us this knowledge were lecturers of the highest calibre, and in a room where many household names in politics had probably sat before us, it was surreal!

Well into the course though, I started have some misgivings about it all and I was beginning to question things. Although the program was educational and it presented a lot of truths, it was a bit polarizing, and only after really looking at what some these lecturers were actually saying, it was very telling and it soon became apparent to me they were just selling one brand of politics, which further inspired me to wonder that if these people were ever to achieve this socialist utopia they yearned for, who would be in charge of it? Because this has been not only the hotbed of debate between all the types of socialist and communist, it has also been the cause of more deaths in the past than all the wars put together.

The 1917 October revolution in Russia springs to mind here, it was virtually a peaceful revolution and although the people wanted democracy the Bolsheviks didn't, and they were the masterminds behind the revolution in the first place and they had other plans. They used agitation to cause in fighting between the provisional governments in place which eventually caused civil unrest, and the Bolsheviks then used this to seize power and stole the revolution from the people, and as a result they crushed all dissent and murdered the Krondstadt sailors who were heroes of that revolution and made it all possible in the first place. 70 million deaths later from starvation, gulags, torture, and firing squads, only then they finally managed to achieve the brand of communism they wanted.

So in trying to ascertain who was in the driving seat of this socialist brand, it soon became apparent to me that it was indeed an intellectual driving force that was behind it (The politically correct one we see emerging today), and it also occurred to me that any input I had to give would never impact on this grand scheme of things that were already ordained, and in reality I would just be another tool (useful idiot!) to achieve something I didn't have a say in of how that grand scheme would turn out. (I had attended some socialist group meetings in the past and I always found a lot of these people were very dull, and they definitely weren't innovators, but seemed to be full of hate, and their vision of life was one of dystopia to me). None the less I decided to badger on with the course and taking full advantage of their education, but only taking out of it what I needed regardless, and besides it was much better than being "darn't pit!"

Although it was my intention to finish the entire course and get a diploma to stick on my wall, half way through my final year something else came along to put a spanner in the works of that notion, when ironically the industrial relations course I was on, was suspended when industrial relations finally broke down between the union and the government in the dispute over the pit closure plan!

But before we get to all that seriousness, I thought a few more stories about ghosts and weird events wouldn't go amiss at this point, just to brighten things up before we get to the next dark topic.

A Few Ghost Stories

And the tales I am about to tell you are those promised at the beginning of the book, they are not hearsay or rumour but actually my own personal accounts.

My first weird experience and starting in chronological order from when they occurred, happened one day on one of the few occasions I was deployed at the back of the pit bottom shaft to carry out the most mundane job in the world of wetting and greasing the tracks to make to tubs go round the bend all day long (me too!). This day we had a shaft breakdown, which meant all shaft coaling had stopped, so in those times when this would happen, I would often take shelter out of the cold wind in a man hole and sit on a pile of stone dust bags (stone dust was in small paper sacks that was used to suppress coal dust from igniting and causing explosions). and this man hole faced the entrance of the old pony stables, and it was where I always got the feeling of being watched and the hair would prickle up on my neck, and that's not all, if I was tired and began to nod off something would often startle me, and sometimes I thought I heard someone whispering near my ear. On other occasions I would be fully sheltered by tin sheeting and nothing could fall from the roof, but small bits of rock would hit me and bounce off my hat. This used to happen regularly, and it wasn't just confined to that area it use to happen in other places as well.

We had a breakdown on a night shift and I just happened to be deployed on a transfer point, so it was only natural to get comfy by lying out on the bench with my helmet over my eyes. There I was drifting in and out of sleep, and again although I was fully sheltered bits of rock were bouncing off me. At one point I thought I could hear footsteps, so the while I lay there I kept my helmet over my face and remained still but listening intently. When those footstep noises got close my intention was to jump to my feet and deal with whatever it was, but when that moment came I was completely paralysed, I couldn't get up and my chest felt really heavy, it was as though something was holding me down, which instantly made me panic, then all of a sudden I was able sit upright again? One explanation could be that I may have just been dreaming and had an episode of sleep paralysis, but in saying that it felt real to me at the time.

There was one particular night shift when I had stopped underground to work over into the day shift, but there was a big time lapse of about three hours before the next shift would arrive on the district, so it was only natural one would take advantage of that little paid bonus by catching up on a little sleep, and so that's what I did. I was actually on the coal face and only about 5 metres from the gate side where I had found a comfortable position, and it wasn't long before I was drifting in and out of sleep, however just as I was getting into the rapid eye movement stage something startled me, and on sitting up to look around to see what it was I noticed that there were lights in the gate, and a beam of light was definitely hitting the Rip (This was the very most advanced part of the gate of an advanced face) so I shouted out to ever it was expecting to hear a bit of the usual banter in return, that usually went something like this: "Gerrup ya lazy overtime pinching bastard get some work done" etc., but there wasn't a peep, just silence. Naturally I then crawled into the gate to have butchers hook (look) for myself, but there was no one there? After hurriedly checking the time over the tannoys with surface control I estimated the day shift wouldn't have climbed in the man riding tubs yet, which meant there was no way anyone else could be on the district? I slept with one eye open after that!

The next weird experience I had happened on a Saturday morning shift when I was carrying out vital maintenance work on a district. There was only a skeleton team working that day and everyone else was working at the main gate end, but I was sent to do a bit of a job on my own on the tail gate Ramming station (This was a tall hydraulic chock that actually sat in the centre of the gate, and when its canopy was pressed tight to the roof girders, and the massive ram on the back was also spragged at a 45 degree angle to roof, it would then be anchored enough to allow the gate chock to push the face conveyor forwards with its ram) but I had a little job to do at the main gate end first, then afterwards had to crawl through the coal face to then do the main job I was sent to do. On arrival at the tail gate my first job was to start the electric pumps that pressurized the hydraulic system that ran the entire length of the face, so now with the hydraulics up and running I went about my work, and despite the fact that I only had the noise of the electric motors and the cavitating pumps for company, and also the fact that I could only see what was in the direction of my cap light beam, and everything else around me was pitch black, I wasn't particularly unnerved or in the slightest bothered about being there on my own at the time, that was until?

I was busy working away behind this big hydraulic gate chock, when all of a sudden with no explanation the hairs on my neck began to prickle up, which instantly made me stop work to have a look around, but after satisfying myself I was on my own, I started work again, hammering and trying to lever this bent locking pin from out of its housing, which was the actual pivot for the giant leg that spragged the roof. When all of a sudden something hit me, and it wasn't a piece of rock or coal, it was a wooden wedge (These wooden wedges were about ten inch long and about four inch wide). I did however spot some piled up on this chock I was working on, and it looked like they had been left there handy for the men to grab when they were setting timber supports at the gate side, so naturally when I also noticed a 1 inch hose that was shaking with vibration from the pumps that was next to this pile of wedges, I automatically assumed they were being knocked off onto me by this vibrating pressure hose? So after I had moved them I returned to hammering away at this awkward bent pin, when all of a sudden in the corner of my eye I again saw another wedge fly past me, which made me jump up and have another look around, but this time convinced that one of the lads had snuck through the coal face and was winding me up, which instigated me shout out the suspected culprits names to tease them out, but after receiving no answer I had another look around and it soon became apparent that I was indeed on my own! Now I was becoming a bit unnerved, nevertheless I soldiered on with this damned bent pin, but now with a little more haste.

By the time the job was done it was near to the end of the shift and all that was left to do was to wait until the guys in the main gate had finished using the hydraulics, then I could knock off the pump motors and crawl back through the face to go back out the pit. In that time waiting although nothing else flew past me, something really strange happened. I saw a light coming through the coal face and it looked like someone was crawling through towards me, but they were still a distance off, so the while I was waiting for whoever it was, I sat behind this big gate chock to shield from the wind and dust that was coming through the coal face. Within a few moments I heard that metal to metal sound of someone's steel toecaps as they hit the surface of the base of the chock, which meant they should have been crawling into the gate at any second, so I called out to ever it was, but once again there was no answer, just silence, so I jumped to my feet to have a look down the coal face, only to find that no one was there. I'm not kidding you I couldn't wait for the main gate deputy to tell me to turn those pumps off, and when he eventually did, by the time he had fully recovered his finger from the button he had pressed to hail me, I had crawled the full 250 metres through the coal face so fast I was practically at his side as he did.

In this next story, although it involves me it was someone else that was nearly frightened half to death.

It was on a night shift and the coal face was stood down because of huge repairs that were being carried out in the out-bye coal bunker system, and there was only myself and a couple of craftsmen and a coal face deputy on the whole district, and this deputy was called Big Red, because he was big and he had red hair. The incident happened after I had completed my work and I had crawled into the main gate to have a crack with the lads (Kill time by having a laugh), and Big Red who actually thought I was barking mad said he enjoyed the banter because I made him laugh. Previously I had been working for most of the shift laid on my back with my head inside the hydraulic workings of the chocks in the middle of the coal face, busy changing relief valves that had failed previous tests, and I was given a certain amount of these to change in a shift by my boss. The while I was doing this some of the other men had to crawl over me several times in the shift, and one being a certain electrician. But later on when I was having the crack with Big Red and the lads in the gate and just as it was nearing time to go home and we were still chatting away (talking bollocks) and I reckon we had been in the gate at least a half hour, when this electrician emerged from the coal face, and on reaching us and him seeing me sat there, he said "how the fucking hell have you managed to do that?" adding, "I've just crawled over you 50 metres back" but when Big Red informed him that we were all here and accounted for he nearly fainted!

Now for the really weird and bizarre, to which I can only describe as an event or some kind of phenomenon. This happened one morning on a coal face that was at the very end of the rail track where the Manrider train actually came to its furthest halt, I think it was South East 4s? And it was around the time we got these new man riding cars which were specifically made for transporting men, and this train could go straight up to the coal face on this particular district. This day I had some work to do on the coal face where I needed some assistance, so I was given a face man as a mate to do the job with me. And because we exited the train in the gate, it meant that we were straight on the job and time wasn't pressing on any work I had to do and there was plenty of time to do it! So I told my new workmate it was going to be a easy job for the two of us and it wouldn't take long, but he became worried that if we got finished too soon he might be redeployed to a shitty job that he didn't want to do, so I reassured him that although it was easy job and it wouldn't take long, I would make it last the full shift by spinning it out, just to keep him happy.

Meanwhile we languished in the gate for a short while to eat a sandwich before commencing this job. When we got started we were both working at the other end of the coal face to everyone else who was working on the breakdown at the main gate end. Our job was to simply use a cut to size piece of timber prop and use it as a sprag when pulling the hydraulic chocks forward onto it, which would then force the Chock over to another anchor position (This was done to space chocks out). My work ethic was to always get stuck in and get the main of the job done first and gauge how much time was left later. I remember chatting away and having a laugh and for once everything was going like a dream, and I was getting a bit worried we might get finished too quick, but we decided to get finished and blag it from there on, and if any of the officials was to crawl by he would only think we were just having five (a rest). We were just getting comfortable and my workmate was just about to offer me a pinch of Doctor Rumney's Menthol snuff, when we heard the face Overman's voice over the tannoy system request our presence in the main gate, and on the double!

On us hearing this we thought it was a work orientated request, so we told him we were still pretty busy, but this Overman now became very insistent, further saying "if you don't come now we are setting off without you", me and my mate just looked at each other thinking it was still a ruse to redeploy him to other work, so we still chose to ignored his request, that is until we had a time check with surface control, which left us both absolutely gobsmacked, we just couldn't believe it. What we thought was probably an hour and half at the very most, turned out to be a full shift, and taking into consideration that myself and my workmate had worked many shifts in the past that had flown by, this was something different, we both recognised that straight away, we had missing time, and ever since that day and whenever we meet, the first thing we say to each other is "duz tha remember that time warp me an thee had?"

Only recently, me and my wife were stopping the weekend in Leyburn in the North Yorkshire dales, and while we were there we took a stroll along what is locally called the Shall's, which is a high path way that goes over a limestone cliff edge that was an ancient roadway, where for many years the Vikings were known to camp in the valley below. We walked for a good hour and half on this ancient road until we came to a gate and a stile where the continuing path looked to be leading off far into the distance, so we decided to call it a day and head back into town and go to a pub, but at a relaxed pace and the same way we came, where we had previously experienced walking up and down several hollow dips and little raised brows in that journey. However it was only after the first hidden dip that we emerged from when we saw that we were already back at the sheep enclosure from where we had first set off, and we hadn't been walking no more than ten minutes! There are lots of theories to this missing time phenomenon and although I've looked into a few of them I still haven't reached any conclusions to what causes it. I'm just hoping that one of the more out-worldly explanations isn't true, in which case I could expect an Alien antenna to pop out of my arse and start phoning home anytime now!

The 1984 Miners' Strike

Firstly there were rumours of a pit closure plan which was leaked by a insider of British Coal who was friendly to the NUM, and although the Government denied the existence of such a plan, the evidence soon mounted as indeed did the stockpiles of coal that was estimated to have grown to at least six months worth supply for every coal fired powered power station in the country. Not to mention the new cable that had been laid across the channel from the French nuclear power stations. It became increasingly evident the government was lying about the existence of the plan when they tore up old agreements on pit closures and refused to negotiate directly with our union leader.

Then came along the biased media who went straight to work on the public by distorting the truth and supporting the government stance at any cost, and they didn't waste time trying to brainwash our union members either by taking advantage in all the moderate areas, typically interviewing miners who supported the union's stance when they were stood inside a pub and after they all had obviously consumed a skin full of beer!

So months of this propaganda went by and when Maggie's lot and the media thought they had brainwashed enough of the public and NUM members in the more moderate areas like Nottingham and Derbyshire etc. She decided to throw down the gauntlet by closing down the Cortonwood Colliery outside of the usual conditions that were agreed in the past. She was banking heavily that King Arthur wouldn't get support for a strike if it went to ballot because the miners wouldn't have the stomach for it, and in regards to whether she was aware that the NUM already had a existing mandate to strike on these actions in place, if she knew or not she must have also gambled that it wouldn't get the support of the whole coal field (so I guess she figured right on that ok!)

I remember the big meetings that took place beforehand in the Miner's Welfare Club that was locally known as the Kibble, which was situated virtually on the doorstep of Sharlston Colliery. The first general meeting was well attended and the concert room was solidly packed with hundreds of men who were overly concerned they might be going on strike, all intently listening to the area delegates put forward the NUM's case for coal, also informing us of what was actually going to happen if further talks broke down. There were a few calls from the floor demanding that there should be a national ballot before a strike went ahead, but this was expected from a certain few, the overall majority there supported their union no matter what! So any notion of putting this to a ballot at Sharlston wouldn't have got much support.

The second meeting though was so rammed full that the emergency exit doors at the back of the concert room and all the windows were opened up so that the hundreds of men that spilled out onto the sports field could hear what was going on inside. There were not only miners in attendance but some of their wives and families too, who were equally concerned and all listening intently as each of these sombre faced union officials delivered the dreaded news of a total deadlock in negotiations and the certainty of a strike, finally leaving it to the branch delegate to deliver the fateful date when that was going to happen, which was March 6th 1984!

Once again the overall majority at Sharlston was in favour of supporting the union regardless, although there were a few calls of protest from the floor, it was once again the same few that everyone knew were either moderate in their politics or they just hated Arthur Scargill, and believe it or not there were a few Conservatives too! There were many wise words spoken at these meetings, spoken from the heart and from both sides of the argument and the arguments were many, but the thing was you could easily recognise those who took their information straight from the TV and newspapers, opposed to those who got it from the horse's mouth, the union! I stayed pretty quiet throughout and was just happy to observe people and try to decipher who was who? This was because we had many pre- discussions at Leeds university leading up to the strike which enabled me to see the bigger picture as to what was really happening, and it was very important to me at the time to try and figure a way to express what I knew in a way my fellow members would understand? I know that sounds arrogant but I think that even with the insight of today a lot of miners still don't understand the full implications and reasoning of why that specific date of 1984 was chosen, and why the unions had to be broken!

Although the content of those meetings was pretty serious stuff, it was a bit of a laugh at the same time listening to all the arm chair politicians spouting economic figures and percentages they had plucked straight from the TV and being so matter of fact about it as well, but it was debate and this is what you do in a civilised society, no one was browbeaten or shouted down at Sharlston! The one thing about all those debates was that virtually overnight everyone and anyone from a lowly Button Man to a mighty Ripper had suddenly become an expert in politics and the economic argument for the case for coal! So I guess you could say it was very educational!

Flying Pickets

Picketing was a legal activity which was an accepted practice under certain labour laws but with stipulated codes of conduct attached, which under industrial legislation ruling allowed those who had withdrawn their labour the ability to convince others to give them support outside their places of work. Although that was the case the use of flying pickets was always contested by the industrialists because it had been so effective in the past, but this time Maggie's lot weren't going to let this happen again.

My first excursion picketing was doomed to failure! We were sent to picket at the Crompton colliery in Lancashire and believe it or not it was already an agreed closure under the old pit closure scheme, and the men there were just tying up loose ends, and no sooner had I found the dammed place, on driving over the entrance ramp the sub frame of my Mini collapsed with the weight of four big miners that were squashed inside! So from day one I became car-less picket, and did I get any financial help from the union, No! But everyone else did. The police in attendance there were Scousers and they seemed ok, and after a couple of weeks we were even sharing food and stories with them and we got on fine.

On our next picket line duty we were sent into bandit country, Nottingham! It turned out to be our Vietnam; we didn't know who was friend or foe. Unlike other towns where we were welcomed and supported, here we could only expect to be reviled. I think this was because on early pickets in the Notts area, agent provocateurs had mingled with the pickets and instead of the men reaching out to the miners in silence or even just turning their backs, it quickly descended into the use of the term Scab and stone throwing, which as a consequence only went to alienate us and cause them to dig their heels in even further, which I guess was the secret services' plan?

My first Picket at Sherwood Colliery was an eye opener to me for a couple of reasons and this was one of them: We were all hemmed in by the police outside the pit gates awaiting the afternoon shift to arrive, and when they did there was the usual pushing against the police ranks as the scabs cars and other vehicles drove past our picket line, and because of the previous altercations mentioned above, new powers were granted to the courts which now meant that if a Picket was arrested he could find himself banned from picketing in the entire area of that particular coalfield. The police even warned us of this that day it came into effect, and just on announcing this two of our own branch union men simultaneously decided to burst through the police ranks and get themselves arrested, which ultimately got them banned from picketing in that area? (in all the time I saw this pair picketing I never saw them push against the police ranks once). What was even more surprising to me was when me and a couple of other guys snuck into the canteen at Sherwood to try and buy some food and something to drink, which was already packed with strike breaking miners, and because of this we just put our heads down and joined the queue. No sooner had we reached the front to get served this women behind the counter suddenly screamed out "Pickets" and she began pointing us out to everyone else in the canteen (Once again the end scene from the film *Body Snatchers* springs to mind here). Suddenly this troop of truncheon carrying keystone cops came wading in, and without any reserve and no matter what we said they relished clobbering us as much as they could, but the really maddening thing about it was that they were the same police we broke our bread with at Crompton!

The mass pickets were the best, miners came from all over Britain in a show of strength and unity for the strike, which should have been very unnerving for the police, but they always knew that the miners no matter how the media portrayed us were in the main law abiding people who were not only in fear of being arrested, but the threat of losing their jobs was also in the balance as well, and because of this the police knew that we were easy to handle. Besides that they also knew that under the reign of Maggie they could get away with anything they pleased: I would like to state at this point that if none of those conditions were imposed upon us, and we had a free hand, we would have been organised and the police would have got their arses kicked good and proper!

It was after one of these mass pickets that I first got arrested and typically in my life it was more like the comedy of errors, because it wasn't very straightforward at all!

It happened one day when my mate had asked me to drive his car to go picketing because he didn't have a license and we needed a car, and in getting me to drive it for him he gained to get a certain amount of expenses for petrol and a bit left over for his trouble. And that was the trouble, not only was it a greedy car which had a twin choke carburettors that guzzled lots of petrol, but in the car owners eagerness to save money out of his expenses, he insisted I only drove it at a mere 55mph all the way to the mass picket site, which at times felt like we were only going at a snail's pace compared to everyone else, who after only a few minutes were long gone down the motorway. Every time I sped up even if slightly by accident he blasted in my ear hole about the fuel and the need to save money, so as one can imagine I got fed up of his stinginess, resulting in us both having a few heated words with each other, which also resulted in me telling him to find himself another driver. No Sooner we had arrived where the mass picket was that morning I went looking for an alternative lift home with someone else, and although I got one virtually straight away, it was to turn out to be a bad move?

When the mass picket came to an end I peeled off with my new ride home buddies and even though there were calls for a drive slow protest on the M1 on the way home, our driver sensibly discounted that idea and he opted to go the A1 route to avoid this go slow instead. However on travelling down one of the duel carriage ways towards the A1, our driver began racing against another car of pickets and basically they were messing about on the road, and the car that got in front of our car in this race, misjudged the oncoming police road block and hit the blue bollards the police used to cordon off traffic for vehicle searches when stopping flying pickets! These bollards had blue flashing beacon lights that fit in the top of the bollards, and now several were scattered in the road.

Without warning our driver pulls up his car and brings it to an abrupt halt, and in that instant he he nudged me with his elbow and asked me to get out and remove this beacon light out of the road and the path of his car, because he couldn't get out of the driver's side for heavy traffic that was going past, so without thinking I jumped out of the car to get this lamp, but when I picked it up the driver then asked me to pass it to him, which I did, only then to see him trap it in his side window pane by winding it up onto it, and when we set off again the driver began making the *Nee-nor Nee-nor* sound mimicking a police siren. So there was me risking my life in the middle of a busy duel carriageway so he can pretend to be in a police car. The first thing I said was, "Are you fucking kidding me I thought this stop was to get this out of the road?" No sooner the words come out of my mouth, we were suddenly T-Packed in by three motorway patrol police cars and pulled into the side of the road. My immediate assumption was that they had either seen our car racing or us interfering with their property. The car was suddenly surrounded by the police who began yanking us out the vehicle without any question and dragging us off into an awaiting police van. Before we knew it we had arrived at the Mansfield police station where the four of us were put us straight into the cells.

The cells were packed full and the one they put us in was a communal cell that had about twenty other pickets already inside, which had a handwritten impromptu notice stuck on its door that read: *Pickets Unprocessed*. And the cells further down had ones that read *Pickets Processed*! Another thing I noticed was that there were policemen dressed as pickets, they were wearing the usual flat caps with the obligatory badges on and *coal not dole* stickers festooned all over their jackets. Once inside the cell I took lead because I had been in these sorts of situations before, as it was very noticeable to me that my comrades hadn't, because they were now shitting their pants and behaving like naughty school boys that were waiting to see the headmaster for the cane. One old bloke just kept repeating the same thing, "I've never been in trouble before", over and over again. They looked like lost innocent children and the driver wasn't so brave anymore. So to put things into perspective and make them feel better I explained the following, I told them to stick to the story which happened to be what I thought we had stopped in the car in first place, which was that the driver noticed an hazard in the road and pulled up and because he couldn't get out, I got out to removed this hazard, and once it was removed we intended to hand it in at the first sign of a police cordon. I also explained that the police are sneaky and might not accept this, so it might be wise to swap our different coloured tops to confuse them. Now with our stories set the four of us sat and waited. Within a few minutes our driver's name was called out and he was taken away to be interviewed, and the while he was away I kept reiterating the same story to the other two and reassuring them that if they stuck to this story the police couldn't make up a charge. I was wrong!

No sooner was I self assured the other two were well versed in our defence and that they would comply, the cell door opened again and we all saw our driver being led back into the cell, but it was noticeable to us all his face was glowing red and it looked like this big six foot 18 stone bloke had tears in his eyes and his shoulders were hunched forward and he was looking down at the floor, which was a very telling sign. Before I could say a word the police officer shouted out my name and now it was my turn, but when he led me away to the interview room I suddenly got a feeling like I have had a few times before in the past when I was a young tearaway and my mates had dobbed me in. No sooner had I sat down the detective told me not to say a word and he went on to tell me every word of the conversation the all the four of us had, word for word verbatim since being arrested, and that my driver buddy was quite happy to tell the truth, which the officer backed up by showing me a written statement of the driver, which stated that it was my idea to get this lamp, he had even told them that we had swapped jumpers. He was so scared of taking the rap (if any was to come) that he had put the blame on me! Why he didn't he just stick to that original story was beyond me. As a result of this treachery the other three were freed and I was put in a cell on my own, but not as a picket, they now said that I was a thief! They eventually charged me with the theft of police property.

I had a laugh while I was in custody though! There I was all on my own and languishing in this cell awaiting to be released, when the police informed me that I might be going straight to court and they may keep me until the next day, so until they made their minds up I was just left there to twiddle my thumbs and gag for a cigarette. Fortunately I heard this voice shout, "Ayup mate have you got a light?" It was coming from the opposite row of cells, so I peered through the square slot in the door to see another detainee staring back at me from his door slot, and after a bit of introductory banter it turned out he was a thief as well, but he had the cigs and I had the matches, so after a bit of quick thinking I got the pages from an old magazine that was left in the cell and folded each page length ways to make them into long concertina strips and then joined them at each end, thus making a fishing rod device. It was about six foot long and when I held it out it bowed, but it easily took the weight of a couple of matches and I also calculated it would easily take the weight of a cigarette on its return journey. I then steadily passed the makeshift pole through the square hole in the cell door and carefully fed it across to the opposite cell. It reached easily and the other guy quickly took off the couple of matches and then proceeded to load up my cig, and after he had successfully sited it, I eagerly but carefully began retrieving it back towards me, practically drooling at the mouth the nearer it got, however just about half way home, this hand suddenly appeared from out of nowhere holding a pair of scissors which cut my fishing pole in two and causing my cigarette to fall to the floor. This rotten copper must have been watching us all the while and had thought it funny to wait until I nearly got my cigarette home! I did see the funny side of it though!

A mock up magazine cover design I made at Leeds University.

Court day

My court date arrived in the post about a month later and strangely enough when I informed the union men of our branch it was touch and go as to whether they were going to support me? The whole predicament took some explaining before they eventually came around to the truth of the matter. It was only then they decided to appoint a union official to represent me in court, and he just happened to be one of the union men who got himself arrested and banned from picketing at Sherwood Colliery. Unbeknownst to us both, when that day came around it just so happened to be the same date chosen for the infamous mass picket at the Orgreave coking plant! For security reasons we pickets only got to know their destinations of mass pickets the very morning they took place, so you could imagine my disappointment, but the union man who was obliged to be my companion was spitting nails at the news he would miss it, and boy oh boy did he whinge, all the way to the court in Mansfield he moaned about it. It turned out a fortunate thing for me really, because the night before I had been squatting with heavy weights in a legs session at the gym and I had only just changed the leg routine, which meant I was really sore in the legs and thigh area and if I had to run for any reason that day I wouldn't have been able to, in fact a ballerina in a tutu could had knocked me over with a feather easily!

In court I told the true version of events and the magistrate thought it was an acceptable explanation, but he went on to say that if it weren't for the drivers own testimony in his statement it wouldn't have even come to court, however after a bit of wrangling between the two opposing councils, I somehow ended up being bound over to keep the peace.

The icing on the cake with this result was that because the police had made this a civil matter they couldn't ban me from picketing haha!

Once out of court and seeing it was still early in the day we both decided to go and see how the mass picket was going on because it was only at the other side of the motorway and one of the alternative routes home.

Arthur Scargill's signature from the Miners' Gala, Thornes Park.

Orgreave

When we arrived at Orgeave it was like a great medieval battle had taken place, there were bodies laid everywhere that were still getting medical attention, policemen and miners were both left sat on the kerb sides bewildered at the intensity of all that had happened. Of course we hadn't a clue what had gone on, so we were bold enough to just walk straight through from behind the police ranks as though it didn't matter, and when we did we could see lots of miners in handcuffs and sat on the floor, and some were getting medical assistance. There were both miners and policemen on stretchers, and walking wounded everywhere, and all looking very tired. The further we walked up the hill we saw the field where all the carnage took place, and it was obvious that some kind of battle had taken place, there were items clothing, banners, shoes, police helmets strewn everywhere, and still people lay where they fell and awaiting medical attention. As we both walked through a scene what looked like the aftermath of Dunkirk, I remember hearing a commotion higher up the brow of the hill and near where the first houses began, and it sounded like the last remnants of defiance by the pickets, so we headed up to see what it was all about. It turned out someone had allegedly taken photographs of soldiers changing out of police clothing, and these squaddies became very nasty and were smashing the camera of the miner who took the pictures, and before anyone else could react and come to their aid, the whole area was flooded with police in seconds, so if there was evidence of that it was lost.

Arriving late on the scene I do remember feeling a slight sense of guilt for not been there in all the action, but also relieved at the same time because like any body builder will tell you, if you overstretch your hamstrings with heavy weight it take at least four days before the soreness goes away and you can walk normally again, so it was a good job really because I wouldn't have been able to get out of the way if I needed to, and as a result I would have probably got locked up or battered by a police baton, maybe both? I had been to a mass picket at Orgreave before and it was the same day Arthur Scargill was arrested and it was splashed all over the news on TV. I was also at the rally in Mansfield where it was reported on the news that he was alleged to have said that he was going to bring down the government!

It wasn't long after this I was arrested again, and believe it or not I was innocent this time as well.

This happened one day when we were sent off picketing and everyone in our car was of a young age, I was about 24 and so was my mate Steve and the other two lads must have only been about 20yr old or so. It was out first journey together and we got stopped by the police going to the colliery we had been sent to and turned back home, so as an alternative we went on to a secondary target to picket, but that was also blocked, no matter which route we took it was useless, so after a while of trying to avoid police road blocks we gave up. On our way back home we entered our own town of Normanton from the north on the A655 and just as we were just passing the police station there, we were suddenly pulled up by this very angry police sergeant who practically ran us off the road in his car. On approaching our driver he immediately demanded to know where we had come from because we fitted the descriptions of some suspects in the same type and colour car that was wanted for a very serious crime. (Bringing this image up to date, it felt like the scene in the film *My Cousin Vinny* where two young kids were going to get fitted up for something we didn't do). No matter what this sergeant thought we had done, with no proof of wrongdoing on our behalf I was confident we couldn't be arrested. That is until this angry sergeant then decided to search the car and in the process he just happened to find a catapult that he said was tucked down the side of the rear car seat (I would like to state at this point I was sat in the front passenger's seat) and on producing it as evidence of wrong doing we were all then put under arrest. Even so, he was only the one copper and there were four of us, so my mate Steve told him to piss off and just walked away, but the problem with that was this Sergeant had already got a hold of the youngest, who just happened to be the registered driver of the car, and he definitely would have blabbed our names, in which case I had no doubt as a result we would have all got our doors smashed through in the middle the night and got truncheoned half to death in the process. So our only option was to go along peacefully with him to the police station and prove our innocence. Once inside and through the electric doors we were all then presented in front of the custody sergeant at his desk, who was a familiar face in our community, in fact he only lived a stone's throw away from my house and he was pretty decent bloke, but then this older policeman came on the scene and he tried to put my arm up my back as though I needed restraining for some reason, totally unaware we had walked into station under our own volition, so I began to protest by saying, "What the hell are you doing, are you nuts?" On this comment about twenty police officers who I think were from Essex and were stationed up here came bursting out from a side room to this old coppers assistance, who then began dragging me about and baring their truncheons and threatening to clobber me, but all the while jabbing them in my ribs, one of them was trying to force me down into a chair, and on resisting him, he was practically spitting the words in my face, "sit down cunt you're in our house now!" They then ripped my cammo jacket off my back and pretended to search its lining looking for weapons, and they did pretend because it had no lining, they just felt the need to rip it apart.

By this point none of us had been told what we had supposed to have done yet, but whatever it was we were made to feel like the Moors Murderers! I also got the feeling these cops were just dying to kick my teeth in. We were all then separated into different cells and later interviewed one at a time. When my turn came I couldn't wait to hear what it was all about? It turned out that we were supposed to have been with a crowd of striking miners somewhere in the Castleford area and entered a Scabs house and battered him half to death. It was all over the news and the media made a right fuss about it, even Ian McGregor the American boss of our coal industry went to visit him in hospital to capitalise on the situation. They made it look like he had been nearly killed, but in reality anyone else with the same minor injuries would have been discharged within an hour after a visit at the hospital, the media just made it look serious, and we were likely suspects! (Someone I knew from another pit got the sack for this incident and he never got his job back).

It didn't take long to convince the police we were innocent of this huge crime, but the fact they found a catapult in the car still remained the same, so they told us we were to be held until they could get to the bottom of it because they were all really keen to find out who it was that kept picking them off by firing ball bearings at them on the Picket line. In my interview with the detective I tried to play it as though I was a law abiding citizen, but this detective was having none of it, and to my surprise he then produced a personal dossier file on my supposed activities throughout the strike up until that date, and the list was really long and in detail. Although he thought it was particularly clever to do this, its contents gave me a good indication of whom the information came from, and that was from certain men that had joined in these activities, but since we had suspected they had indeed gone back to work. After the interview I was put back in a cell and left to stew, and in the hours that went by they even told us we could be kept another 48 hours. So I took a chance by asking the detective if I could confront my mates while he was there to convince him that if I told the guilty party to cough up he would, to which this detective agreed. He gathered us all in one room where I put that to my other car mates that if the guilty party was among us they should cough up? But it was no big surprise when no one did! Nonetheless my actions was enough to convince this detective that we were genuine and he also agreed that the catapult could have been put in the car at any other time, and within the hour we were all finally set free. *Phew!*

Normanton cop shop.

If Things Couldn't Get Any Worse

The news of the first men to attempt to break the strike at Sharlston was horrendous, and like all bad news it went around the town like wild fire that the police had been seen measuring up the roads to the colliery entrance, which was the usual indication the police were methodically planning their strategy to enter the pit premises. So much was the revulsion the word of an unofficial mass picket also spread like wild fire too, and an angry mob soon assembled the night before the expected incursion was to take place, and just after midnight when all the pubs had shut this determined Mob converged on their beloved colliery site.

Everyone and anyone who could tagged along even if they were in the industry or not, just to make sure Sharlston Colliery became an impenetrable fortress to stave off the influx of potential scabs! Barricades were soon made by pushing empty coal tubs down to the colliery entrance to stop the scab coaches entering the pit gates, and within only a few minutes of this being done the police dog vans had arrived on the scene, but they were to no avail because the pickets were particularly angry that evening and at the first sight of these unwelcome visitors, they were met with hail of stones from the Mob, who's mood was such, that if police had released their dogs it was very unlikely they would have returned back to the van again, and realising the gravity of the situation the police then quickly sped off to get reinforcements.

When the news of police reinforcements came everyone was stood behind the barricade and were just waiting around, when all of a sudden a fellow Picket came running down the pit stack from where he had been posted on look out duties and he was shouting the alarm that the police were on their way. On questioning this out of breath Picket as to how many there were, he just blurted "thousands of them" (or did I just pinch that from a scene in the film *Zulu*? No, it definitely happened that way!) Within minutes this army of police turned up at the pit gates who quickly flooded the area and set about dismantling our barricade, and because the pickets were easily outnumbered everyone took off into the surrounding colliery buildings to fight a guerrilla style war from there. To combat this, the police sent in the riot police and dog handlers to flush them all out, which they did by letting police dogs off their leads, forcing all the pickets to scatter and fall back behind the colliery premises to regroup.

For months after that first incursion at Sharlston there were gangs of pickets roaming the dark streets at night and the mischief was a plenty! It was like being at war, there was a constant police presence and they had even mounted search lights on the pit head gear to scan the whole area, and fully laden vans packed with riot police regularly patrolled with their spot lights searching every shadow.

On one of these night manoeuvres the main focus of the pickets was to erect road blocks at specific points to stop the scab convoy getting to the mine, but without endangering life of course, and as a precaution some lads even went to the lengths of getting road works beacons and road closed barriers. A few individuals just went and did their own thing and they were basically unaccountable to the majority of the pickets, so other things may have been done outside the knowledge of everyone else. The union never encouraged anything outside of peacefully picketing, and these guerrilla-style tactics were usually instigated by those of a higher conviction to the struggle.

This particular night about a hundred men split off in two groups, each group prepared to erect road blocks at certain locations, but when one of these groups was making their way to the potential site and using the cover of the hedge rows of a the small country lane to get there, they were suddenly compromised by a police van that came over the hill, which then stopped at highest view point and its search light then began scanning in the direction where everyone was, which left the pickets no choice but to hit the deck and lay down as flat as pancakes below the long grass cover. So now all these men were now laying silently in the grass waiting for the police to go, but when the police van began moving again it was only going about 5 mph and all the while its search light was carefully scanning the area where everyone was in the grass. No sooner the van got dead level to the pickets, it suddenly stopped, so it was vital that everyone stayed dead still and really quiet. The van was now so close the pickets could even hear the policemen's actual conversations inside, which meant if the pickets could clearly hear them, they could clearly hear the pickets if they made the slightest sound.

Unfortunately one of the Pickets was in so much of a hurry to hit the deck on the sight of the police van, he had inadvertently dove straight into a huge pile of dog shit, and now he had dog shit all over his brand new sheepskin coat, and the smell was so bad it was making him gip, and he couldn't hold it back any more, and he began to make weird gipping noises, but because he was trying to silence as much as he could, it sounded so funny that everyone was straining to hold back the laughter, especially when he whispered, "trust me to find a dog's nest... gip... gip... *yeeeerrp*". All of a sudden the conversations in the police van fell silent when they heard this strange sound, and they were now looking in the direction it was coming from. Then a copper's voice was clearly heard explaining to his fellow officers "It's just a fox having its leg over, I should know I'm a country boy I hear it all the time", and on that conclusion the police van just drove off, but leaving all the lads rolling in the grass holding their ribs with laughter at the sight this lad desperately trying to rub this dog shit off his sheepskin with a sod of grass, and gipping all the while he was doing it. Every few seconds and after he thought he had finally removed it, he kept sniffing it to check and every time he did, it was usually followed by that same gipping sound that just kept making everyone laugh.

One of the best laughs I had on a picket line was at Allerton Bywater Colliery. It was the very same day a lorry driver was dissuaded from crossing our picket line, but he had to go onto the colliery premises firstly to turn around, unfortunately on his way out he accidentally ran over a policeman's foot, and believe it or not the police actually arrested him for it and there was big trial afterwards! This day a small group of us pickets were walking around the colliery cricket pitch when we stumbled upon a few big clumps of magic mushrooms, which to the bemusement of the older guys who hadn't a clue why, me and couple of mates began picking them. The funny thing was that one of the lads was eating everyone he picked and I don't think he realised how much they would affect him in the end, he probably thought that because he was a big lad and drinker he was impervious to them, but by the time thirty minutes or so had passed by the full magical effects hit him he became an absolute nightmare on the picket line, and eventually someone had to drive him home, but later in the miners' institute it was said that they couldn't get him off the pool table to play pool because he was laid on it with no shirt on, pretending to be an upturned beetle and he just kept laughing all night long!

Mass Picket at Sharlston

It was about three months after the very first of the strike breakers had actually crossed over our picket line when we heard the news from the union that it was our turn to have an official mass picket at Sharlston Colliery. Although it was good news some of us pickets thought it was long overdue, because since that early incursion of scabs travelling in one solitary armoured police van, the numbers of scabs now willing to break the strike had increased so much that the police had to use two armoured coaches to fetched them all in. The more this treachery began to rise so to did the state of apathy in the men whose picket line they were now crossing. So the news of a mass picket was a welcome one even if it was just to boost morale and put on a show of unity. But not only that some of us thought it was a chance to finally be able to outnumber the police for a change, and perhaps foil their plans to get the Scab convoy onto the pit premises.

So all expectations were high and everyone was hoping it was going to be a huge turnout that would take the police by total surprise and as a result they would be overwhelmed by our numbers, and because this was our back yard and we knew the local topography of the landscape like the backs of our hands, we were sure we could outfox the police and breach holes in any perimeter they tried to throw around the colliery site.

However that wasn't to be, when the Mass Picket day came it wasn't as massive as everyone had expected. Although there were a lot more people there than usual, it was nowhere near the size of the Mass Pickets that we were used to and instead of the five to ten thousand in attendance there was only about a thousand people. It was a big disappointment to some of us not only to find that it wasn't that well attended, but we also found out it had been purposely organised on a smaller scale and limited to the few that was invited, such as local dignities and trade union councils who had brought along their trade banners to show us support etc. There was also a foreign news crew and a couple of local celebs in attendance too. Apparently the word on the ground was that the Mass Picket was purposely toned down on request by the local union branch because they didn't want their small terraced housed community that was in very close proximity to the colliery site, being engulfed by thousands of Pickets who would have come from all over the country, and it possibly turning into a battle ground like we had seen in other villages the past.

So I guess the plan was to keep this mass picket a dignified and a low key one (A sensible decision!). But that idea was doomed to failure from the start, because as soon as the word went out on the drums about our big push at Sharlston, it again spread like wild fire and as a consequence it became an open invitation to almost anyone who was sympathetic to the miners' cause, which unfortunately attracted a few rough necks that came along just to have a go at the police. And because I knew some of these people and they had arrived at the same time as me, it was automatically assumed by some of our union men that they were all my responsibility? One of them even called me over to tell me that he was overly concerned about their presence there, and he also warned me that if anything untoward was to happen I would get the blame.

There was at least hundred of these extra helping hands that came along unofficially invited, and what most of them had in common was that they were all still pissed from the Sunday night session in the pub, and because some of them had never seen a picket line before, I think they just reacted in the same way as they had seen from small video bites of miners clashes with police on TV. As soon as this crew landed they pushed their way straight through the crowd of about a thousand people that were already peacefully picketing, and went straight up to the police line and began kicking their shields and attacking them with pieces of paling that they had torn from the colliery canteen fencing. On seeing this, the head union man came straight over to me and put the total blame on my shoulders for fetching what he described as an unwelcome rabble! Even though they weren't my responsibility I couldn't ignore the situation especially after hearing this union man and everyone else's concerns, so I immediately went to calm the situation down and rein them in a bit. Eventually I managed to herd them right back to the crossroads of Cow lane and about 50 yards at the rear of where the official Picket front line, and where I thought they would be out of harm's way, but I was wrong? By the time I had achieved this it was too late, this crowd of my so called thuggish mates had already caused enough havoc to rattle the police's cage and now were determined they were going to do something about it, and unbeknownst to us actions had already been set in motion!

The while we all stood at the crossroads everyone was deliberating what they should do next, some wanted to go home and others wanted to stay, but as they were discussing what to do one of the guys just happened to notice some suspicious shadows making their way across the colliery stock yard and in our direction, which could have only been the police, so as a precaution everyone in this group dropped back even further up this lane just in case the police were trying to sneak up behind us. No sooner had we all relocated to what we thought was a safer place, about 50 of these riot police with the long batons and round shields suddenly came bursting from between these terrace houses like hornets from a nest with their batons raised and they were determined to crack some nuts. On seeing this everyone scattered and split in every direction to escape, some jumped over fences into the allotments to get hidden in there, and some others ran down the opposite lane, I and a couple more lads ran up the hill directly away from the mine.

Unfortunately though at the exact time these riot police tried to ambush us lot from behind there was also coordinated assault from the police ranks at front which was designed to trap us in on two sides, although the group they were after managed to escape, all those who had just been stood peacefully Picketing got trapped in-between, and as a consequence those who couldn't get out of the way got a good hiding from the police. Even the few who thought that it was safe by seeking sanctuary in the miners' institute the Kibble were pursued inside and they all got clobbered too!

In the meantime I and a few others that the police were keen to get a hold of were still being chased up this road which ironically is called Hell Hole Lane! And because I was wearing my big boots and heavy coat I was blowing really hard and nearly running out of breath. So I decided enough was enough, and I wasn't going to run anymore. I pulled up and looked back to see who was actually on my tail chasing me, only to see that it was just one persistent copper still making the effort, and his mates must have peeled off chasing someone else, now leaving this copper all on his own, so I just stood there and waited for him to catch up, but when he got to about twenty yards from me he looked around for support and when realised he had none he quickly did an about turn and swiftly made his way back towards his fellow policemen.

The end result of this whole fiasco was that I got the blame for fetching all the thugs along and was the cause of our sacred club getting stormed by police and a lot of nice people to getting beaten up! But I will say it once again I didn't fetch them, I had no control over anyone that day.

I admit I wasn't squeaky clean and I've often walked in the grey areas as far as picketing rules were concerned, but getting the blame for things I didn't do followed me throughout that period of the miner's strike, so it was no big surprise! I will admit when it was me, and it was me who painted on the Kibble wall entrance, JOIN THE PICKET LINE, NOT JUST THE PARCEL QUEUE! because every time we got back to base from a long days picketing there was hardly anything left out of the food parcels that were donated, because the people that joined the parcel queue for food easily outnumbered those who actually went out picketing. (Looking back in hindsight I think it was probably wrong to do that.)

The strike went on longer than everyone expected and it was now a case of just holding out, but all the while the striking miners were hoping the rest of the country would see what was really going on and the real reason behind the destruction of the British Coal Industry. But the problem was then as it still is today the media was totally biased and they would not tell the truth, which not only went to aid and abet every move the government made, it also gave Maggie's henchmen the confidence and green light to do whatever they wanted to do to us, even allowing the full apparatus of the state to be set against the striking miners. But to do this they also had to demonise and vilify the miners' reputation to turn the public against us.

From the start the government's propaganda machine went to work and within only a short period of time it had managed to dirty the reputation of these heroes of WW1 and WW2, who were once honoured by the whole nation for their war effort, and endearingly named the Backbone of Britain and the Salt of the Earth by reducing them now to The Enemy Within.

To achieve this title the government and police and the media worked together to destroy the reputation and good character of honest hard working men, and this is how low they had to stoop to do it!

Firstly they began at the source of Maggie's sudden rise to power by blaming the NUM and their past wage demands for being the cause of the infamous winter of discontent which got her elected in the first place. Then they tried to make out that all the miners were communist and we got our orders straight from Russia and we were actually a militant paramilitary movement. To reinforce these notions the powers that be had instructed the police to only arrest pickets who were wearing camouflage jackets or pants, and afterwards their pictures would be taken and displayed as evidence to back these allegations up on national TV, knowing full well that most miners wore this type of clothing for fishing and shooting rabbits and of course ferreting! I know this for sure because I nearly succumbed to being a victim of this myself, and once it was recognised what they were up to it was highly criticised by the NUM at the time!

We were sent to a mass picket at the Annesley Colliery in Leicestershire where there were at least 10 thousand in attendance. When the scab convoy arrived I was pushing against the police shields as they approached the colliery entrance, all of a sudden my cammo jacket was grabbed from behind and it was being held tight by someone that was pushing me, at first I thought it was a fellow striker giving me a boost, on glancing around I noticed it was a couple of older blokes who had the usual clothing and flat cap and badges. Then without warning the police shields opened up and I was purposely pushed into the hands of the awaiting police. Fortunately I was too quick for them when I stealthily sidestepped their clutches and in an instant I took a flying leap straight over the heads of the police line and back into the rank and file of my fellow miners. No sooner I had managed to escape I spotted the same two blokes that had pushed me from behind, but they saw me at the same time, and no matter how many times I shouted for everyone to stop them because they were uncover police, no one reacted quickly enough to feel their collars for a change, and they managed to just disappear into the huge crowd of pickets.

That very same day on the teatime news they presented a picture of a line up of men that were arrested that day, and surprise, surprise they were all wearing camouflage gear, and straight away the allegations were made that these miners were a part of some organised paramilitary group. All just timed right to accuse King Arthur of having dealings with Libya's ruler Muammar Gaddafi, they even mentioned something about him sending weapons to the miners, and believe it or not they had somehow got a NUM insider to corroborate this.

There was another trick the police and the media used, and usually when it was a mass picket, the police would infiltrate the rank and file of pickets and at a pre-organised time, as soon as the TV camera crews were ready, and after they had given the signal to go ahead these undercover coppers (army boys?) would then start charging at the police shields and throwing stones! I know this to be true because I witnessed these tactics several times, especially after all the pickets were warned of these practices, it was easier to spot and they now stood out like a sore thumb, and on the few occasions they were even challenged by the official pickets, they usually slivered back into the police ranks. I'm not saying all the stone throwers were the police, but they did sometimes instigated the initial stone throwing and if the police had previously given the pickets a hard time, it was obvious the pickets would join in. This is exactly what happened that day at a Selby coal mine when the hail of soft muck that was thrown from the farmers field at the police, it was later described as rocks when presented on TV. There were many instances of collusion between the government the media and the police, and these three were the real axis of evil in that struggle and again just like they are today!

Coal Scrumping

Up until the 1980s just about everyone in the coal industry had a coal fire and although many were switching to gas for convenience, in the main everyone depended on coal to heat their houses, so when this supply was cut off the only thing left to do was to either burn wood or go out looking for coal. The problem was that to get coal you either had to steal it or mine it yourself. Stealing it was the easiest option and this was done by either sneaking in to a power station and taking it from the stockpiles or likewise stealing it from stocks of coal that were still left on the colliery surfaces before the strike. At one of the power stations at a certain time in between the hours the workers there clocked off for the day and the night security clocked on, there could be as many as 200 men who had parked up and hiding in the hedge rows waiting for the exact time to go and plunder, and when they did they would swarm out from the surrounding trees from all directions with their shovels and sacks at the ready to dive straight into the huge piles of coal, where they would begin shovelling like mad to fill their sacks of the precious black stuff. The workers at the power station knew they did this but I think they had sympathy for our cause because they often tipped coal where the striking miners couldn't be seen taking it.

Mining it yourself was another story, this meant finding a seam of coal that ran near to the surface and then it was just a case of simply digging it out, but the problem was that the seams near to the surface weren't usually rich in coal content, although it burnt it made a poor fire, it was more like what we called slag, which was half coal half sedimentary rock. There were some seams of good quality coal but they were scarce because they had usually been already extracted by years of open cast mining. If you were fortunate to find one though, they usually went from the surface in a downwardly direction further underground, so the more coal that was dug out the deeper the hole got, and without proper mining equipment and safety precautions in place, it could be very dangerous, as all of us miners at Sharlston were to find out when we sadly lost one of the lads mining for a bit of coal for his fire. I won't go into detail of that incident out of respect for his family, but I would just like to add that he was one of the nicest men you could ever wish to meet and he was respected by everyone in his community. God bless him rest in peace.

We lost another good guy who was a larger than life sort of character and a personal mate of mine. He was always fun to be around and likewise I have never heard a bad word said against him or he himself speak a bad word about anyone else, and again he was liked by everyone. This poor lad died while queuing to get the donated hand outs in the food parcel queue in the miners institute, he wasn't that old but he did have a health problem and perhaps the stress and humiliation of having being reduced that present situation might have caused his clinical condition to finally kill him! God Bless him rest in peace.

There was another type of coal seam and this was found in the old railway train yards, where over decades the coal train's buffer used to smash together and the coal would either spill from the top pile or any holes in an unrepaired coal carriage which eventually formed a layer of coal on the ground. If you could figure where each of the railway lines used to be each side of the track would be a rich vein of not only coal but also coke and anthracite too! These rich seams could be up to 1 foot thick and at least 3 feet down, this was because they would have been buried by ballast over the later years, but when you hit them it only took minutes to fill your sack with coal. This particular coal site was in Normanton and it was plentiful, it saw a lot of people throughout the whole of the strike, there was enough for everyone and within only a few months of coal scrumping the sight from the railway bridge looked more like the trenches of WW1 than a old rail yard.

On one of these coal forages my Dad who was also on strike insisted on accompanying me and my older brother to prove he could still pull his weight and help to support the family, so we both reluctantly allowed him to tag along, but I will never forget that day as long as I live. When we arrived at the dig there was a least 40 other people already there and seeing that this small group of Scrumpers had already bagged their lot, they were quite happy for us three to jump in the spot that they were vacating. My Dad then enthusiastically pulled up his pants and took command of the shovel we had brought in the wheelbarrow, and headed towards this trench hole, but to get into this trench he had to step down from higher back fill that the previous diggers had discarded, and because my Dad was wearing his bifocal glasses that distorted his downward vision, he misjudged his footing and fell head first straight down the trench. Normally I would have found it very funny, but to tell you the truth I was a bit embarrassed for him, because there were lots of other coal Scrumpers there who saw what he did and they couldn't believe their eyes either, and the funny thing was that no one laughed, me and my brother just looked at each other shaking our heads. It was just like watching a scene from a Laurel and Hardy film, and very typical of my Pappa.

There was another source of coal which came from the last place anyone would have ever expected? It came from our pit manager! He had hired a Barrel Washer to clean the un-washed coal stockpiles that still remained on the surface of the mine, purposely in order to get coal to the pensioners in the area, and I guess he must have also sympathised with the striking miners' plight, by always making sure there was a fresh pile of coal tipped in the car park of the institute every day, not only coal but logs from the stockyard too, which was not only a very kind gesture but it was also a very brave thing to do, because it certainly would have got him in to a lot of trouble if the senior executive management had ever found out!

The amounts of charity and support we got from outside the industry were fantastic, it was overwhelming at times, and it came from everywhere. A good example of the local support we received was we went collecting in the high street one day, we filled our collection buckets easily in no time at all, nearly everyone in the high street including most of the shop keepers were more than happy to contribute, although there were a few exceptions, some shopkeepers openly refused by stating that they didn't agree with the strike, but these people were typically either Conservatives or brainwashed stupid by the TV, so it was no surprise to hear this, but it was a big mistake in a mining area, because the word went out and their trade suffered after taking that sort of attitude. Regardless of the few, in the main we got fantastic support, and for everyone come out for us like they did, lifted the hearts of every striking miner to continue with the struggle.

It was a struggle indeed, especially for those striking miners who took no heed when warned about taking on unnecessary debt and overstretching their incomes, which made them dependent on overtime to meet their bills. These folk suffered more than others and they were worrying times for a lot of people. Some were lucky enough to land temporary jobs that paid cash in the hand; in fact some even stayed in those jobs and never returned back to the pit. Others weren't so lucky and they were unable to get that bit of extra money and therefore they lived in abject poverty and despair throughout the whole strike.

It got so desperate that some of the younger miners even broke into our own welfare shop and stole all the contents of thousands of pounds worth of goods to sell them on for much less to money, just to put food on the table!

So it wasn't surprising when each week the strike went on we would hear the rumours of other miners breaking the strike, and week by week the rumours of those numbers grew and the word on the picket line began to spread that even some of the more famous heroes and big hitters of the mine had gone back to work, but again this wasn't surprising news either because we never saw any of these guys on the picket line, so it wasn't a big shock that some of the big money men might be just thinking about their own pockets! Another rumour was that one person in particular would stand at the side of us all shouting scab as the convey went through the gate, and after everyone else had peeled off home this guy would then go in to work?

What really shocked me was the skulduggery that was going on at my local colliery. One afternoon nearing the end of the strike I was visiting my Mum, when we both heard a knock on the back door, on my Mum opening it there stood the very same guy who had many years before come bearing the belated bad news that I had been in a underground accident, but this time he was bearing a different type of news! My Mum shouted me to the back door and on seeing this guy the first thing I noticed was his body language which was the first indication it wasn't a social call, because he was acting a bit timid as though he was nervous about what he was going to say, and no wonder! I couldn't believe my ears when I heard the message he had come with this time! He told me that he had been sent directly with the word of the pit manager to inform me that he had received a dossier from the police of all the alleged extracurricular activities he thought I had been involved in throughout the strike up until that date, and on that basis of evidence he was going to sack me if I didn't return to work straight away!

This was very strange, why did an NUM member from my coal face but from another shift come with this message? Was he strike breaking? He wasn't a union man, so what was his role in this? As for the alleged dossier it probably was the same work of fiction I was presented with in the police station months before. This was nothing less than a ruse the senior management had manufactured to try and break the strike. The local management must have been ordered to do this because it was repeated up and down the country and they were hoping that if the likes of me were scared back to work more would follow, but like Bugs Bunny always used to say, "dey don't know me very well do dey".

I've never been a grass or a traitor and despite my rough edges and sometimes cavalier attitude to things, I always try to hold the sword of righteousness and the beacon of light and truth, so you can guess what I told him to tell the manager to go and do, and a few more swear words too, I also gave him the message that if he wants to sack me based on a load of bullshit, tell him good luck!, With this finite answer this bloke then took with my reply. But what a cheek and a nerve though, hey!

It wasn't much longer after this when that fateful day came that drove the death knell into much of the sympathy the striking miners once held with the majority, when a death actually occurred. It was the day when some silly sod decided to drop a concrete block from a bridge onto a car and killed a taxi driver who was taking a scab to work! I knew from that day on we were finished, and it was the bad news the media were waiting for, who wasted no time to revile us again in the eyes of the rest of the world.

To make the situation worse a large block our funding was stopped when one of our very own Labour leaders talked the major donors out of it!

By this time the union had exhausted every argument and were now on the back foot repeating the same arguments in our case and although they were still based on sound economic reasoning, we were losing the extra public support we needed, which just went to show how fickle the public can be!

To show an example of this and how the public's heart strings can be easily pulled and manipulated to swing their opinion, you only have to study the whole argument presented both by the union and the government at that time.

The Government's view of the industry was based purely on economics, but all their economics were based on heavily subsidised coal and electricity from other nations and although it was cheaper it was got by unfair competition, and here begs the question how long would that cheap supply last? All coal produced was given a spot price in Holland and it was based on all coal that was available no matter where it came from. This is where the stock market price for coal was set regardless of how heavily subsidised it was or how it was got even if it was through slave labour, it was still available and it drove prices down. So on that basis the government were not only going to close down the coal industry, but they were also willing to destroy thousands of jobs connected to coal mining as well. Not only that they also knew it would devastate hundreds of communities, putting millions on the dole. The amounts of people in engineering and manufacturing industries that were connected to mining were now going to close, all because of a short term set price for coal, it didn't add up then but it all certainly adds up today doesn't it!

The union argued the obvious and that was to keep modernising the coal fields and run with the old agreed closure plan, which would keep people in work and create money. In the meantime modernise the coal fired power stations by introducing fluidized beds that would enable them to burn coal without pollution, and keep our state asset for generations to come, so we would never be short in the production of electricity and we would always be able to stay independent!

No matter how well these points of view were put across and how truthful the miners' case was to see, in the light of all this new negativity that was brought on by the taxi drivers death, we were still seen as a militant tendency that was trying to overthrow a legitimate government by many!

I think it was around this time that the NUM made a fundamental mistake by playing the government at their own game, they should have instead used the economics argument differently, perhaps the only reason they didn't was because their own socialist dogmas were preventing them from supporting this point of view.(we were fighting for jobs and the right to work) If you take into consideration that we the NUM members were not only fighting for our jobs, but also the ones of the members of NACODS and all the staff and management as well, who in the main only got their job because of the numbers of men working at the collieries at the time and the NUM demanding better health and safety and training etc! Another point to be taken into consideration was the fact that the original management structures descended from the old coal owners to fill the pick of the jobs in the new NCB (National Coal Board) who then created jobs for the boys with open cheque books from the government of the day. As a consequence of this being allowed happening, the senior management structures were overloaded at every level to make their own jobs easier, and it was this situation that made their spending get out of hand and as a result it made our coal too expensive!

For example: Sharlston Colliery had a manager, assistant manager, deputy manager, deputy assistant manager, four under managers, nine colliery over-men, 12 underground face over men, and about 60 underground deputies. And virtually the same structure repeated in the mechanical and electrical, health and safety, dust, and training departments. These structures continued right up to the area level where the management executive had chauffer driven cars and ate in their very own banqueting suite with silverware and service. The top honcho there was rumoured to be flying about in helicopter, so God only knows what went off at the British Coal headquarters in London.

The point that I'm making is why didn't we the NUM use the argument that most of the above weren't needed based purely on the capitalism's own economics, and seeing as these folk didn't seem to be bothered about fighting for their own jobs, why didn't we throw them to the wolves in our case? Why didn't we shed them as the dead wood in our economic argument? I know it was murmured from the floor of the rank and file many times, but I never heard it uttered at national level to support that very point of view. To argue these points watch the documentary about the last months of Kellingley Colliery: The men there didn't need all that top heavy management! And to put it plain and simply as everyone knows, it has always been the case that there are always more chiefs than Indians!

However that case was never fought and from then on the end was nigh!

The March Back To Work

It was the 3rd of March 1985 when it was decided by the NUM that we should all return back to work and although we hadn't won our case we weren't defeated, we went back to work on our own accord, we were still determined to keep up the pressure with our case for coal, and no matter how soul destroying it was we were still determined to march back in to work with dignity. Nonetheless some of our union branch leaders couldn't help but make a pig's ear of that! When we got the date to all return back to work it was understood by everyone that there was going to be a dignified march back to work, but the management structures in the higher echelons saw this as an act of defiance instead, and they did everything possible to disrupt this march back, and they were nearly successful at some pits, including Sharlston too! I think this happened for a few reasons, I also think it could have been sanctioned by our branch leaders? Firstly, when all the active pickets rang up the miners welfare some were told the march was at 6 am and others 8 am and some were even told there was no march at all, which was very confusing. So I turned up at 6am to tell those who had turned up to hold miners back for the march at 8 am, but on arrival the lockers were full of scabs that were cowering and skulking about, and there to give them support was this assistant manager who was shouting at the miners that were stood around in the lockers, telling them to hurry up and get down the pit or be sacked. This idiot even began shoving people around and acting really aggressive, obviously trying to show how unafraid he was in front of us thuggish pickets. To counter his instructions I was doing the exact opposite and telling all the good guys to hold back, but totally ignoring all the scabs, when this assistant manager got right in my face shouting "if your bannering get off the premises you're all sacked", meaning if we wanted to march into the pit in dignity behind our branch banner we would lose our job! So we politely told him to fuck off and to get his arse out of our lockers and when he saw that we meant it he did!

At 8am a large majority of the men were assembled in the field at the back of the Kibble club, all ready to march back in behind our banner. It was then a couple of the union men took it upon themselves to give a heartfelt speech before we did. But to mine and just about everyone else's huge surprise, which was expressed by the loudness of the discontent, this head honcho union man then announced that because we all went out on strike together we should all return together, meaning scabs as well!

On hearing this statement I was shocked and horrified! It was not only a betrayal of the highest order but in that very instance it suddenly dawned on me that whoever gave out the wrong times for the march back to work to all the regular pickets, could have purposely done it in order to keep certain people out of the way so the scabs could peacefully join in the march back to work? And things were about to get even worse! After we had all proudly marched back into work behind our banner everyone was just left hanging around and no one seemed to know what to do next, so I went to try and find some union men for some leadership, but they had suddenly vanished into thin air! I even went to union office to check there but it was locked. In the short time I was gone everyone who was still hanging around waiting for instruction, suddenly got one when a message was sent from the manager's office that instructed everyone to start picking up litter around the pit top, and they were told their names would be taken later for attendance to get paid. But this was nothing less than a humiliation exercise and when I glanced up at the office windows I saw that some staff were eagerly taking photographs of men picking up litter, and it wouldn't have surprised me if some of the union men were there also, so on seeing this for what it was myself and others walked off in disgust.

Pit Closures!

It wasn't long after this march back to work that the government started implementing the very same pit closure plan they had denied all existence of throughout the strike, and the pit closures came quickly. When the first of the mines were closed those who wanted to take redundancy took it, and them who wanted to stay in the industry were usually fitted in at other collieries. The designated collieries where they were to go had to make room for them coming, so the management of these collieries encouraged all their unwanted workforce and bad attendees to take redundancy to get them off the colliery books, but what was offered in payment at the time was poor, although some took this initial redundancy offer, it still wasn't attractive enough in the main.

I think Sharlston made room for men that came from about four other pits that were closed down under this program, and mainly from the neighbouring Ackton Hall Colliery, the same colliery I had attended on that infamous school visit.

Ackton Hall was known to be a militant pit by everyone, and I think that because of some decisions our union men had made in the past, some Ackton Hall men may have previously held the name of Sharlston in low regards, and it must have been a bit of a blow to those to have to come to such a moderate pit, but a more of a relief to others? There was a rumour that when our manager used to be the manager at Ackton hall he got to know the men well, and because of this he knew who all the troublesome ones were, so he only selected the ones he wanted before any came.

When the first influx of Ackton Hall men eventually arrived underground, it was almost funny to see some of them reluctantly trudging towards the manriding cars to start their first shift, they looked absolutely dejected and really gutted to be there, which you can sort of understand because they had spent most of their life working at Ackton Hall!

I distinctly remember these four guys that climbed into the same compartment of the manrider as me, and on noticing their expressions they all looked close to tears, then I heard one of these guys say "Thuv shut wrong pit thanoz", and on this sentiment his mates and a few others sat near, all replied in unison "Hi, thaz rate there", "Aye, thaz not wrong... Aye". They weren't all sad about having to come to Sharlston though, some thought it was just a bit of a change and others really wanted to come because they were fed up of not earning any bonus in their pay packets, whereas at Sharlston they could. One enthusiastic little chap marched straight up to me with the biggest grin on his face and looked highly delighted to be there. He was small a stocky and probably in his 30s, and when he approached me his hand was already outstretched for me to shake, but when he introduced himself he said, "Hi, my name is Boo Boo, everybody calls me Boo Boo". On hearing his introduction I couldn't keep a straight face, me and my mates just cracked up laughing, we couldn't believe how serious this bloke was wanting to introduce himself as Boo Boo! We laughed all shift long about it and by the time I saw him again on the pit top in the showers, my ribs were so sore they hurt just looking at him.

The Ackton Hall men came with a reputation and there were many negative stories of their militancy and work to rule attitude, whether it was true I don't know?

The most famous rumours was that if was a hot and sunny Monday morning the pit would typically receive a bomb scare just before the afternoon shift started, as a result the entire workforce would then end up in the beer garden at the local pub! Another tale was about this underground team that was supposed to build this major junction, but they managed to spin it out to about three years, and every time the under manager visited to see how they were getting on, he would always leave shaking his head and commenting on how disappointed he was. Therefore they were affectionately afforded the name of the Disappointing Gang by the manager at that time. But these were all rumours and Chinese whispers, and in fact they weren't a detriment to Sharlston at all, after they came they proved their worth and in only a short period of time the whole colliery achieved its first million tonnes! And guess what? We all got a mug!

The Mug Story

On receiving my celebratory silver mug I saw it for what it was a token gesture only, and no sooner I got it home I consigned it straight to the back of the cupboard with disdain while making the comment of how worthless it was to my wife. Then one day weeks later I made the same comment while sat in the riding cars underground waiting go out-bye and home, when this know-it-all mouthpiece suggested that despite my lack of regard for this tankard, I was full of shit and it was more likely that the said mug would be polished up and mounted with pride on my mantelpiece! So sensing a few easy quid I bet this bloke £20 it was still in the box in the cupboard, and so this bloke took me up on the bet. But in the car park before we set off home this guy caved in when I offered him the chance to come to my house, and he welched on his end on the bet. On arriving home I entered through the kitchen door and the first thing I noticed that the box the mug had come in was now on the kitchen work top, and on glancing into the living room I saw that my wife had just finished polishing the mug up and had lovingly placed it on the mantelpiece!

It was never the same again

I think the weirdest thing about coming back to work underground after a whole year was all the pit mice had gone! They had all starved to death, which must have meant that these mice must have lived all those generations surviving only on the food that men fetched down the pit, and although they were a bloody nuisance for the smell and pinching our snap, I missed them, somehow it wasn't the same without the mice!

This reminds me of another story, about this bloke who was absolutely terrified of the pit mice. It was rumoured that when he was a young lad and he was playing out late his Mum used to have to shout him in to get a bath before bedtime, and because he didn't want to go in and he still wanted to play out, he used to go and hide in the corn field at the back of his house, forcing his Mum to have to ferret him out. On one of these occasions it was said that when he was laying low in the corn field hiding from his Mum a mouse ran up his shorts!

Knowing this we made up a rumour about one last remaining mouse that was a giant mouse the size of a cat that had only survived because it had cannibalised all the other mice, and we also added that it had been seen on our district and it wasn't scared of humans because it had already attacked someone who was having a shit behind a conveyor belt and this poor bloke had to fight it off with the shovel he had taken with him to bury the job! When we were telling him the story he was sniggering and laughing it off as a joke all the while, but later when he was on his own further down the gate he was nervously jumping about and screaming at every noise made when a lump of rock that fell from the roof.

Union Elections

I had lots of misgivings about our union leadership at branch level for a number of years and all throughout the strike, but these last few events took the biscuit and a lot of people were disillusioned, especially me and I wanted to make a change.

At the first opportunity I put up as candidate to be a union representative and won selection after receiving a large vote in my favour, which I believe must have slightly worried some of the senior union men and management at Sharlston, because if I was to become too popular I might be bold enough to stand for union secretary the next time around. And they would have been right!

However that wasn't allowed to happen, from day one it soon became apparent that some of the union men and management were going to ignore me and try to scupper anything I tried to do by subtly sending me to Coventry!

And here's how I think it was done. At the first union meeting after I was elected as a union rep I brought up an issue under: Any other business, which consisted of me addressing the chair and informing the meeting about a group that had helped the miners throughout the strike who were now asking for our assistance in their own struggle by showing our support and sending a delegation to their rally with our banner as a way of thanks, and all it would have taken was a small amount of money for petrol and a bite to eat for each of the four men delegation that was usually sent with the banner to push it. To my disbelief the motion was out rightly dismissed with the argument that the strike was over and done with, and that we needed to leave those sorts of things behind us now? On hearing this attitude I went into platitudes pointing out our moral obligations and the need to get our priorities right! The chairman's reply to this was "I'm not having a newcomer come here telling us all what our priorities are we've done with all that, and we need to build up our welfare fund again" and while this head of the chair was spewing this ungrateful mouthful, I was looking around the room for a bit of support, and knowing that there was two known left wing union men at the meeting I was sure I could at least count on their support, I think one was Marxist Leninist and the other a Stalinist or something, but they stayed as quiet as two church mice. So this was the attitude I was up against.

The next spat I had was when I brought up the poor choice and quality of the food that was on offer in the pit canteen, which I thought was of a low standard for the prices we had to pay for it. The explanation we were always given for this was that our canteen was in a system that worked like a cooperative in the pit canteen catering business, which therefore meant we subsidised other canteens with smaller turnovers, and whereas the bigger collieries had full menus of cooked breakfasts and dinners, we were limited to a choice of a few different cold sandwiches, a bacon sandwich, pork pie or sausage roll, and besides the obligatory beverages of tea and coffee and a few types of chocolate biscuits to dip in, that was it! So my pitch was that we wanted a better standard because there were now lots of young lads who were into their sports and training in gyms to keep fit and healthy, so they needed to be a better variation of nutritional choices on offer, and since our canteen wasn't set up to cook meals we could still improve the menu by adding things like fresh fruit and salad and perhaps healthier wholemeal bread and others such things like that. This was also shot down in flames by the chair who immediately dismissed my point of view with a range of arguments as to why nothing could be done. Fortunately there were a few other attendees present that had come along to the meeting to give me support in a show of hands and as a result this motion was carried and it wasn't long before a wider choice of food was on offer in the canteen.

Regardless of that small success it was later to become blatantly obvious to me that no matter if I intended to be a responsible union man and do my best I wasn't going to be given that chance, and that realisation came to me soon after I was invited to attend my first underground safety visit. One of the other duties of a union representative besides being a mouth piece for the men, was that they were also obliged to attend safety visits as a delegate from the union to accompany the management and staff of all departments on their weekly safety visits all around the colliery site to ensure everything was safe and up to standard. And on those visits each official had a responsibility to make notes of any hazards or to make suggestions of improvements etc. The main concerns were about accidents caused by tripping, stumbling and falling and other things like guards for around moving machinery and anything else that needed to be checked around the mine. Nevertheless no matter how diligently I filled in my reports on those inspections and how many suggestions I had made, when it came to the monthly meetings in the conference room with the manager in attendance, none of my reports were ever discussed, they had been purposely left out. I also began to notice the manager would not look or speak directly to me. On another occasion I was told I had to attend a monthly management consultative meeting with the personnel manager, but on entering his office the Personnel manager said, "That was a brilliant meeting thanks for your input, good day sir"! So being confused at this situation I walked straight over to the union office to tell them what had just happened, and when I told the union men there they just laughed at me and said they were astonished I had actually turned up for it.

I'm not trying to be Peter Perfect here, but I believe that if someone has been elected to represent the workforce they have been put in a position of trust, and if those structures of the industrial relations that were put in place to ensure a good working environment were being abused, it would go against my integral way of thinking, so I didn't think it was right at all.

My next falling out was when I started highlighting the fact that the underground diesel Locomotives weren't safe and that the diesel fumes they exhausted were choking the men when taking them in and out-bye of the mine. Although this air pollution problem could be made better if the flame traps of the locomotive were cleaned every hour, it wasn't kept up with because the Loco teams were kept too busy, so it was a problem and in raising these issues I was accused of trying to close the pit down. I feel this was because that if our pit sustained any more need for new investment; it might have put it in the red and on the list for closure. Sharlston had the capacity to produce good cheap coal but getting it out of the mine was a problem, whereas other pits had drifts with conveyors belts that went right to the surface, which meant they could produce more coal because they could get the coal to the pit top easier. Our system depended on two shafts and the coal had to come up in skips or coal tubs that Loco diesels had to fetch from in-bye, which was a lot more labour intensive and it made our profits only just above the border-line that kept the colliery in the black.

The airborne dust was another issue I was concerned about, especially on certain districts where the coal seams that were being cut contained a layer of shale that ran through the middle. This was because shale produced more dust and the more cutting machines that were in use the more dust was created. Water was used to counteract this but if too much was used on these districts all the mechanical equipment would get bogged down and sink into the soft floor surface, so it was a problem!

(Airborne dust is the finest particle of dust that floats in the air rather than falls to the ground and is the size of particle that easily gets trapped in the lung).

This particular day I was working in the tailgate of a district that was very dusty and the while I was there I saw this guy whose job it was to site the dust monitor machine, who would then stop with it until the end of a shift and then he would take it to the surface to be analysed by the dust suppression department. The results would then sent to the area headquarters for assessment. (Or the other way round?) But when I noticed him surround this machine with thick white sticky gauze that was made to stop dust called Bondina, it instigated me to enquire as to why this guy was doing this? Although I had noticed this practice in the past and I had challenged the dust suppression guys on this matter before, I was usually fobbed of with some officially made up reason that I wasn't expert enough to challenge. However this time being a union man I felt empowered to get to the bottom of it once and for all, as a result me and this guy had a bit of a row which ended up with me pulling this sticky gauze curtain down, which instigated this dust suppression guy to get straight on the phone to report me to his boss.

On coming out of the mine that day I was met by a couple of senior union officials on the pit yard, and it looked as though they had gone to special effort to wear their suits to look more official when they told me they wanted a word with me in the union office. Once inside the office they put it to me again that I was trying to close the pit down, to which I could only repeat slogans that were written in bold capital on the signs that everyone saw when they entered the pit gates, which said "SAFETY STARTS HERE" and "SAFETY IS NO ACCIDENT" and argue the very point that the long term health issues caused by dust and diesels fumes were not excluded from the overall safety campaign in the mining industry.

But it fell on deaf ears because I believed they actually thought I was only raising these concerns just to cause trouble. So on realising the reality of the situation, it only left me two choices, I could either to take the matter further by officially reporting it to the highest levels of the NUM and the health and safety executive or call for a general meeting to make sure everyone knew the situation. But both of these could have resulted in me been responsible for the actual closure of our pit based on health and safety grounds, and that definitely wouldn't have gone down well with the workforce at all, I would have been lynched! So instead I decided to mention the dust situation to as many of my fellow miners as I could to try and gauge what they thought about the matter, and what should be done about it. After doing so it soon became apparent that most of those I had informed, had like me also noticed the dust monitors being surrounded in sticky Bodina sheeting, and they had already assumed that the reason for doing this was indeed to tamper with the real dust level results, but they just took it as an accepted practice if they wanted to stay in work!

It is very important to say at this point that not only did I seek advice from the Sharlston men, I also sought it from other miners that worked at other collieries in the surrounding areas, and in doing so I found to my huge surprise that covering the dust suppression machines with Bondina sheet was common practice at some of their collieries as well! So taking this set of circumstances into consideration, the very fact that the miners were willing to forgo their own health in order to stay in work and keep their community together, doesn't this unselfish act in itself bear testament to the truth of why the miners' came on strike in the first place, and totally opposite to what the biased media would have you believe, that the miners were militants hell bent bringing down a government?

Voluntary Redundancy

It was around the end of 1988 and British Coal were now more desperate to get rid of men, so they increased their offer of redundancy, which now had the added extra bonus of ten thousand pounds to the thousand pounds each man already got for every year he had worked. Although it was only on offer to those at the collieries British Coal wanted to close and the dead wood to make room at other pits, it still wasn't on offer to the general population of workers at Sharlston as yet, as it was estimated our pit still had at least ten years of life to go. Regardless of that not many would have taken it anyway, because it was barely six months wages to some and what use would that have been? They would be still out of work, so in effect it was just like an advancement of the dole money!

By this time I was well into my second year term as a union representative and by then I had become totally disillusioned with working in the industry, so I then began looking for work elsewhere and on mentioning this fact to the landlord of the pub where I sometimes worked on a weekend as a doorman, he offered me chance to become a publican, but he said I needed some capital to start with. So regardless of the fact that in my past I had fought for jobs, and despite the fact I was still a union man and it would be frowned upon, not only by the NUM but also by my workmates to go against all those very principals, I decided that under these circumstances I had had enough. The reason for my disillusionment was the realisation that no matter if I stayed on as a union man or even if I got elected as the union secretary the reality remained the same, I still wouldn't be able to change a thing because everything that could be done to keep fumes and dust to a minimum was done, and other than the colliery getting a sudden massive amount of investment to modernise the mine, which was highly unlikely, the situation wouldn't change, and taking into consideration that if I was to remain there I would have to breath in all those diesel fumes and eat all that dust for the duration of my mining career, it wasn't a choice I was willing to make.

Throwing in the Towel

I decided to throw in the towel and because redundancy wasn't available to me at the time, that towel was in the form of a very patronising letter to the pit manager, the very same manager who couldn't even bring himself to speak to me or look me in the eye! In that letter I praised him for his kindness for giving aid to the miners throughout the strike and there was some other ego massaging stuff about how fair he was and how much all the lads liked him etc, but in reality it was just to butter him up so he would allow me to leave the mining industry, but with a full redundancy payment, which I now needed to fund my new career. (To be truthful I could have written any old load of rubbish in that letter and he would have signed it gladly. I remember commenting to the missus on its creation, saying that the manager and the union branch officials might even put a bonus on top.)

Believe or not the very next day after handing the letter in to the manager's secretary, I received a phone call informing me that my application for redundancy had been accepted and within an hour a taxi was dispatched from the colliery in the form of a pit minibus and it was already waiting outside my house, which then took me straight to the union office where I was eagerly greeted by the union secretary at the time. I will always remember the big grin on his face, he could barely talk for trying to hold back his laughter, it was as though he thought something was hilarious about my redundancy request and I was wondering why? Then all of a sudden I saw the source of that laughter when he produced the very same letter I had handed in personally to the manager's secretary. On producing this letter he was grinning from ear to ear, obviously smirking at the letter contents, possibly thinking he had got something over me, but then he went on to tell me that the manager had called him over to ask him what he made of it, to which he then told me, in fact he was more than delighted to tell me, that he had told the manager to let me go because I was a red and that they wanted rid of me as well!

If I hadn't have been so desperate for that cash to get out of mining, I definitely would have slapped the smug look from this bloke's face, but to be honest it slightly shocked me and it took me a bit by surprise, because I didn't really consider myself a lefty or a socialist at that later time. I thought I had made that clear over the years that I just saw myself as someone who demanded fair play and to do what was right! And now I had to take this sort of insult from someone who I thought fell well short of the standards of a good union leader. Instead of making a scene I kept my mouth shut and took my redundancy papers from his hand without saying a word, because I had got what I wanted and that's all that mattered to me. When I walked out of that office it felt about two stone lighter, it was as though a great weight had been lifted off me and I practically skipped down the road to the awaiting pit van taxi, and I couldn't have been any happier!.

Little did I know at the time that in the later years I was to return back to Sharlston, and it definitely wasn't to mine coal!

Publican

My first pub was in Bradford, this was because I had a criminal record for fighting on a licensed premises in the past and the local licensing sergeant wouldn't allow me to hold a liquor licence in his jurisdiction, which meant I had to move further afield to an area where the police weren't that strict, but it was understood that if I proved myself over a number of years without incident, he would then allow me to hold a license in the Wakefield area.

However talk about coincidences, to get my licence I firstly had to be interviewed by a local police inspector, but the funny thing was that this inspector was newly promoted from being a detective, who just happened to be the very same detective who questioned me in the interview rooms when we all got arrested in Normanton.

When I opened the front door to see him standing there I nearly died there on the spot, luckily though he didn't recognise me at first, but a little later on in this interview when he got on to discussing my previous occupation and the fact that I was an ex-miner, he wanted to know what my feeling were towards to police since the miners' strike, and before I could answer, I think the penny dropped, when he suddenly broke out that conversation and said, "didn't I arrest you in the strike?" his face immediately began straining and his eyes were searching in his head trying to recall where he knew me from, fortunately with a bit of quick thinking I managed to furnish him with his recollection of me by giving him an alternative occasion when I had met him, and this was about six months before this interview.

I was sat in my car in the town centre and waiting for my wife to come out of the shop and in a place which was allowed for pickups only, but definitely no parking, when I saw this detective who was walking the beat with a young new copper and it looked like he was showing this rookie the ropes. On this detective spotting me waiting in a car where I shouldn't have been, he urged this young cop to go and deal with me, all the while he watched over him as he gave me a telling off. So before this inspector could figure out where he had originally seen me, I gave him that memory instead. Although he seemed to accept this explanation I could see that his mind was still trying to remember where else he had seen me, because he kept the same wrinkled brow on his forehead since that very question. Nonetheless he left my house happy with that explanation in the end and I eventually got my first licence and pub.

My pub career was a short one though, because once again the government of the day saw fit to interfere in this industry too and before five years were out and under recommendations of the Monopolies and Mergers Commission, they managed to tear this industry apart as well, as a result it put everyone's livelihoods working in the trade was in jeopardy, and the whole uncertainty of where the industry was heading caused the closures and loss of many tenancies in the pub trade, thus leaving me no option to find other work.

Back to Square One

At first I was determined to never to return the pit again, so I sought work wherever I could find it, but well paid jobs for unskilled workers were scarce and the only alternative was labouring on building sites, but again that didn't pay nowhere near to what I was used to. After a couple of years of working a week here and a few month there and spending half my time chasing employment, so it wasn't long before my savings began to dwindle away and I could no longer manage financially. I had to do something about it but the only other alternative was to do the unthinkable, and that was to go back down the pit, and the only way I could do this was to go to work with private contracting companies.

Having decided to do this I applied for a pit passport which would allow me back into the industry if my training was up to scratch and my health was tip top, which meant having a full medical and a paid search for my records and only after I had fulfilled these requirements I was issued with my pit passport. Fortunately that same week I managed to get some work with a small mining contracting company in Castleford, who set me on as a Chock fitter to work on a coal face contract in the Barnsley coal field at a pit called Houghton Main. That was only the start of it, from then on I went on to do just about every type of job there was in the mining industry, eventually to become what was to be the crowning achievement of my entire working career underground and that was a Dosco driver! Which doesn't sound much under British coal standards because they wouldn't be under as much pressure as contractors would have been, they could afford to let anyone have a turn at driving a machine, whereas in contracting a Dosco driver had to be really good to keep his job, he not only had to be fast at cutting the tunnel profile, but he also had to be very tidy and neat and keep the tunnel tight to its measurement and direction, a most importantly he had to achieve the maximum advancement of the tunnel each day.

I got my first taste of Dosco driving at the Prince of Wales Colliery and it was on the recommendation of a site agent of that same firm, who I had previously worked for on another contract at Askern Colliery in the Doncaster area, who thought I was a good worker and a potential foreman. But it was a very shabby introduction to this job, because I was introduced as a potential foreman, and some of the other men that had been there years were quite resentful of me walking straight into a heading job that their mates were already promised. So it was a pretty uncomfortable beginning in that sense of things, and because of this it seemed as though some of them wanted me to fail, but on top of that the conditions couldn't have been any worse for a trainee driver. The mud on the ground was at least a foot deep and the floor was so soft the Dosco tracks would sink into the ground causing it to get bogged down and making it really hard to manoeuvre the machine, so to counteract this wooden battings had to be laid on the floor every time the machine advanced forward, which was an added frustration in itself and very tiring to do. Not only that, the dust was so thick in the air that the driver couldn't even see the profile of the rock that he was actually cutting, therefore it could only be managed by someone with lots of experience of cutting blind, which I didn't have, so it was hopeless to expect the trainee driver to do the job effectively. To make things even worse, water rained down on us all the shift long and it was like working in a shower, but this water was white and it burnt our skin!

Because of these conditions and the tunnel team's eagerness to earn money it was only natural that they didn't have the time for a trainee Dosco driver to learn the skill, which meant they were reluctant to let me have a go, and they would only let me drive the machine every now and then when time wasn't pressing, because of this I only got to cut the tunnel profile a couple of times in that whole training period. Despite these set of circumstances, believe it or not I still managed to get my papers to say I was fully trained on the LH1300 Dosco at the end of it? When the first opportunity arose for a new team to be assembled to start in another contract heading the company had won, they said they were satisfied with my performance enough to put me in a new team in a brand new heading as a second driver of the Dosco. So from then on it looked as though things were looking up for me and I hoped that soon I would become a big earner!

Unfortunately another spanner fell into the works of that notion when I was actually using a spanner one day. I was taking some belt structure bolts from out of some brand new belt structure that had just been installed in a new adjacent heading, and this was because we had no structure bolts in our heading and we urgently needed some for our structure as it was advancing forward, while the heading I was taking them from was still being prepared. As I was doing this I was spotted by a company foreman who began to ridicule me for taking the bolts from out of the freshly built structure and witnessed by all of my team mates, even though it was the logical thing to do because the bolts could have been replaced at a later time, but this foreman got a bit too insulting when he called me a Wanker! So as one can imagine it ended up with me having a bit of a heated disagreement with this foreman! And as a result it also ended up with me getting booted off the job!

In my time while I was contracting I had to stick up for myself a few times, because it was a brutal line of work and the men were not only tough and rugged, but they could also be backstabbing cheating dogs as well, which meant that sometimes disagreements could get really heated and even end up being settled physically.

Fortunately I was only out of work a day when I was lucky enough to hear of a job vacancy on a new contract at Rossington Colliery in the Doncaster area, but it was for Dosco drivers only. Although I hadn't much experience I jumped at the opportunity and rung them up straight away, and after lying through my teeth I had managed to convinced this contracting firm that I was a dammed good machine driver,and again fortunately I got the job. On arriving at Rossington Colliery the tunnel heading I was sent to wasn't quite ready yet, so it gave me plenty of time to familiarise myself with this new machine, which was a MD 1100, and because it was a smaller machine than the LH 1300 Dosco, it was more manageable. Luckily this tunnel was well ventilated, which meant the dust would be at a minimum and visibility would be good, and because the floor hard, when we did actually set off tunnelling I was well acquainted with this machine and it was a piece of cake!

After only a short period of time I became pretty good at driving the machine and I was soon beating the other shifts advancement for the week, which after a while of doing so I guess it got me a bit of a reputation as a top Dosco driver for that particular company, which was solidly endorsed when the Rossington contract came to an end, and whereas the company had to lay most of the men off, they kept me on the books and sent me on to another contract they had at the Kellingley Colliery instead. Where on my first shift on nights I managed to cut out and set five rings compared to the usual three the other shifts did, and when it came to building junctions, even though I had never done it before, we were beating the other teams at that too, so a in short period of time I managed to win respect of my employers by breaking a couple of shift records for tunnel advancement, which put me in good stead and from then on my machine operating skills were in demand by at least two private mining companies, which made me secure in the knowledge that I could walk into a job with them at any time: I suppose to any young miner at that time I had perhaps become one of the big hitters to him in his day.

Mining contracting was a tough industry that housed a dog eat dog mentality within its workforce, which meant there was always someone lining up ready to take your job and even stab you in the back to get it. The foremen knew this and they took full advantage of that situation, and they could be really mean as well, not only would they sack someone if they thought that they weren't good enough or slightly slacking on the job, but they would sack someone just because they didn't like them.

I was the Dosco driver and charge hand in this particular new tunnel heading at the Riccall Colliery in the Selby coal field, and we had an Irish foreman but he was mean, so mean he sacked two of my tunnel team mates because they laughed when one of them accidently stood on his hand while he was on a makeshift ladder. He approached me at the end of the shift and said "say goodbye to your workmates they won't be here tomorrow" then he added "you're ok", so on hearing this I asked him why? His reply was that they weren't good enough!

The first thing I did when I got out the pit was to confront the site agent about this foreman, even while the foreman was actually there, I told this site agent what the truth of the matter, but the site agent backed his loyal foreman and he wouldn't reverse his decision, which made me really angry at them both, so I gave him a right colourful mouthful, and told them to stuff their job up their arse. On exiting the site cabin I got straight on the phone in the pit baths and on my first call I landed another job, and to top it off, when I saw the two lads that were sacked earlier they told me the site agent had changed his mind and decided to keep them on but on another job instead!

Contract tunnelling was a tough job, but I liked it, you got respect and you could earn a good wage, but only those willing to work hard survived. There was no tolerance for absenteeism and there was definitely no rest days, and you were expected to work when the company told you to work, when the bosses cracked the whip everyone was expected to jump, and that was because they generally paid a very good wage.

(This is a typical example of the work ethic and mentality of the contractors of old, those who had been in the game for years before the pit closures began. One day when I was working at the Prince of Wales colliery in the same tunnel that rained white burning water on us, and I was cleaning up the floor to site the leg of an arch the Dosco had hoisted from the ground and while I was shovelling away knelt on my knee pads, a lump of rock the size of a breeze block fell from the roof and struck me on my pelvis bone just above my buttocks, the sharp edge of it snapped off leaving a piece of rock stuck in my back, and when my work mates pulled it out it left a hole two inch wide that began to bleed a lot. Although my work-mates administered a bit of first aid, my hip was numb and it really needed some proper medical attention! Be that as it may, when I told my fellow heading men that I was going out of the pit early to get it seen to, the Foreman and the rest of my contractor buddies thought I was a big softy and were very surprised at me for going home. That's how tough they were).

Type of Dosco. ©NCMME

A square tunnelling machine. Contains public sector information licensed under the Open Government Licence v3.0

A machine driver's job

A typical Dosco driver's shift started in the surface site cabin, where he would get to know the underground conditions and the advancement of the tunnel from the previous shifts and from that information the team would calculate what they may need to take underground with them. From then on it was a mad dash to get to the job as soon as possible and by the time the men got there everyone would be stripped down and reduced to wearing their shorts and knee pads only, and if conditions allowed they would commence tunnelling straight away.

A tunnelling team usually consisted of four men, but that depended on what system they used. In the old way of tunnelling an arched shaped profile of a metre deep would be cut out of the rock and coal and a steel arch that was originally in three sections would then be assembled and set in place, which also would be secured to the previous set ring by the use of Tie bars. The arch would be then covered in with corrugated sheet and after being pinned tight by the use of timber and wedges the tunnel is extended.

The more modern method of tunnelling was much cheaper and a lot simpler, which totally did away with the use of heavy steel roof supports, instead of tunnelling a profile of an arch the tunnel was cut Oblong Square! To do this a different type of tunnelling machine was required, which unlike the Dosco had a big wide tank like boom with a rotating drum of teeth of the end of it. The Leigh Norse was totally different, although this machine was about the same size and ran on tracks its cutting head was a wide drum of teeth that raised up to the

Dosco at work.

height of the cut, which in one downward motion towards ground level would cut out the perfect oblong square profile and after the collectors on the front of its conveyor had cleaned every morsel of fallen rock up, it would then pull back to allow the team to start securing the open roof. This was simply done by pinning a long piece of thin steel sheet across the entire length of the freshly cut roof, which had five pre-drilled holes. Through these holes four men would use two roof bolting machines called Wombat's to drill the roof and secure these straps upwardly by using 9 ft bolts that were put in the holes after pills of quick set resin was inserted, they would then be pushed up to the roof in a spinning motion until the steel sheets that were called Watchstraps were pinned to the roof, and hey presto the roof is held up!

This system worked by eliminating what the geological engineers call the Cathedral effect which relied on holding the pyramid shaped area that was directly above the tunnel square in place, thus using the bedrock to keep its shape to hold itself up. But the worrying thing about mining like this was that if there was ever a huge geological movement in these types of gates they might collapse. So to make sure we were safe and we could detect any movements it was stipulated that every 30 metres of the roadway a test bore hole was to be drilled up into the roof strata. The bore hole had to be 10 metres high and inside a clip device would be inserted to the top of this bored hole to hold a plum line that hung down to the base of the hole where a Tell-tale plum-bob was hung. This was a small reflective tube with three colours running around it which were the same colours as a traffic light and at the bottom of this plum-bob it was set at green at exactly the roof level. If one day you noticed it was on amber you kept an eye on it, but if it was on the red it meant danger, the higher strata had dropped and the Cathedral affect was failing! This happened a few times, but when I informed the deputy of this he just altered the string and put it back on green again.

This reminded me of a tale that everyone must have repeated at sometime in their life about a bloke who had noticed a red warning light that kept coming on the dashboard when he was driving the car and it was bothering him, so rather than taking it to the garage to get the problem fixed, the bloke removed the bulb out of the warning light instead!

None the less I felt safe in my work and for once everything was going good for me and I was looking forward to a prosperous future.

Doom and Gloom

Unfortunately it was on one of these total bolt installations at the Stillingfleet Colliery in the Selby coal field that I worked my last shift underground. It was just when I was about to hit the big money and me and my team mates were just setting the very last piece of steel roof support before we then went on to the total roof bolt system, which would have meant lots of opportunity to make large wages of around £1000 per week! The trouble was that when we were hoisting into position the steel support fell from its holding place on the machine cutting head, which left me no choice but to go and lift it back on again, but as I went in front of the cutting machine to physically lift it from the ground to reinstate it, the unsupported area of roof it was going to support that was now directly above me began to make serious cracking noises, which was a bit of a warning, but eager to get this girder back in place I held onto it a while longer to allow another man to drive the massive cutting bed underneath it. But when the next loud crack came the roof came with it as well! Although I dove for cover under the Leigh Norse for shelter as quick as I could, the pile that came down was about twenty tonne and a huge rock struck the bottom of my leg and broke it.

So there I laid underneath this cutting machine and trapped in by this huge fall of rock from the roof and in the short while I was waiting for my workmates to dig me out, all I could do was stare at my bent leg, the very same one I had bent all those years ago and think of all those times my Dad would say to me that I should have stayed at school and got educated and then I could have applied myself to something better instead of going down the pit, all those wise words that fell on my stubborn deaf ears. Then came the shock, but not the shock of injury, I was used to getting injured by this time, it was the shock of the realisation that I was going to be out of work a long time and miss out on all that lovely money I could have potentially earned, and it was this that upset me the most. It also occurred to me that it was yet another narrow escape and it could have been a lot worse. It was only few months previous when a large junction roof girder fell from its cradle when I was lifting it into position with the Dosco boom head, which slid down the boom of the Dosco towards me and if it wasn't for a slightly upturned bolt on the machinery that it got snagged on, it definitely would have chopped my head off! So these were sobering thoughts!

It took three and a half hours from the time of the accident to getting me out of the pit, which wasn't surprising because anything to do with me is never straight forwards at all. Firstly the men had to dig me out, secondly and believe it or not a stretcher couldn't be found on the district. Once one was actually found they decided to load me onto the flat blade of an FSV (This was like a big diesel that ran on tyres and instead of two forks at the front it had a wide flat steel platform that lifted up and down just the same) and when we actually got going on the flat bed of this FSV, both me and the stretcher came off twice because it was a long bumpy ride, and the men had to keep loading me back on again, which wasn't very reassuring at all.

The worst thing about it all was the poor attitude of the ambulance crew that were waiting on the surface to take me to hospital. On seeing my condition they said that my leg that was now really swollen wasn't even broken, but was just badly sprained and because of this on the spot diagnosis, they didn't treat me as an emergency and they wouldn't put the siren on to get me to hospital quicker, as a result of their ignorance we got stuck in a traffic jam in the city centre of York. All the while I was in agony, and they just kept sarcastically saying "You will be alright there's no hurry". When we eventually arrived at York Hospital this ambulance crew must have downgraded the alarm with the awaiting hospital staff, because they just sat me in a wheelchair and shoved me in a walk in shower cubicle and told me to clean myself! I was black as the ace of spades and in agony, and I couldn't understand the poor concern. I remember thinking it was very shabby of them to leave me to do this. After my x-rays returned though, that level of concern altered as soon as it was found out I had six breaks in my tibia that would need reconstruction by the use of metal rods and screws, which now meant what I thought was going to be a short stay, actually ended up being five weeks in York District Hospital.

The one thing that struck me after spending all that time in hospital was that because I had been in an air conditioned environment for the whole of that time, when I stepped out outside for the first time the smell of petrol fumes and pollution was so overwhelming it made me feel really sick, but my Dad and my wife who came to pick me up that day couldn't smell anything out of the ordinary.

Once at home it was a case of just waiting for the pot to come off and then after some physiotherapy learn to walk again. Although I needed to be out of work a while to fully recover I was once again pestered out of my convalescence to go back into the workplace by the mining company that employed me, who I think were probably worried about having to pay out compensation which accumulated the more time I had off work. And because I wasn't fully fit they offered me a job with light duties, which just happened to be on a new contract they had just won, and this was to fill in all the pit shafts of all the closed collieries in the area where I lived, which was more than handy and to my surprise they were the shafts of Nostel, the Haw park ventilation shaft, and my old pit Sharlston Colliery!

A Shaft Fill Supervisor

This new title was afforded to a bunch of us after we had received a short period of instructional training, which included slideshows of the do's and don'ts and lessons that had been learnt in the past from the mining archives and other up to date literature on the matter.

Surprisingly it was more technical than I had imagined, there were quite a few implications to doing the job correctly and lots to take into consideration beforehand. A rough explanation of what the job entailed would be: Firstly the pit shaft as to be cleared of all structure, cables, pipes etc, then just below the water table level in the shaft, the walls would then have to be dug out wider to except a concrete plug, which would be poured once the shaft below was filled with rubble to that level (This work was done by men that were used to working in pit shafts and they were lowered down in a giant bucket called a Cradle) and once this was done the shaft could be filled to the top.

The shaft had to be filled centrally by the use of a chute that was carefully positioned over the hole, this was to avoid the shaft fill rubble hitting the sides of the shaft: (A) It could hit the shaft walls causing them to collapse and stop it being correctly filled (B) The velocity of the brick rubble dropping hundreds of feet and hitting the shaft walls could cause sparks that would ignite any methane gas that may be present in the shaft which might explode, causing the shaft to act as cannon and fire its contents up into the air and wrecking all the roofs of the nearby housing estate (This lesson was learnt after it actually happened twice in the past history of shaft filling).

When the fill was compacted up to the water table height a wet concrete plug would be poured to seal off the workings below, as soon as it was set the next stage was to drop about 60 tonne of puddle clay down the shaft that would splatter on impact on the newly installed concrete plug to create a water tight seal. This seal had two purposes, it stopped old pit water and methane gas rising upwards from that point and it also prevented the natural water table above from getting contaminated from the workings below.

Nostel Colliery had two shafts and a drift that came direct to the surface, and this was the way their coal came out on a conveyor belt. Haw Park was just a single ventilation shaft that was in the middle of the lovely Haw Park woods and it was an absolute pleasure working there. This lone shaft was capped off but not filled and it had a gas vent chimney on the top. It was often the case that the local boys had learnt how to throw up lit pieces of paper to light up the gas and sometimes a twenty foot flame could be seen that used to light up the night sky in that area.

At Sharlston we had the two main shafts and an old ventilation shaft that was already capped but also had to be filled in. All the while this heavy underground preparation on each of these sites was being carried out, I was afforded the luxury of driving the minibus or pit van until it was time to start actually filling the shafts. It was a right Bobbie's job, the cushiest job I've ever had, and I was kept on full underground money too! Other than taking men to their job sites and nipping the bosses about, I spent most of the time mooching around the Sharlston Colliery pit top (mooching means rooting about, rummaging in places I hadn't seen before).

It was an eerie experience to walk around completely deserted places where I had remembered so much activity in the past, but looking on the bright side of it, I finally got to access all the places I had never been and often wondered about in my years working there. There was still a few colliery staff left behind to supervise the health and safety aspect of the work, so the main offices were still out of bounds to us, but everywhere else there was an open door, or if it wasn't we had the keys to open the doors. (Boot/Crowbar).

What really shocked me was the amount of valuable equipment that was just left there lying around, and even though it all had been put on the market for other working collieries to come and take their pick, there was still enough stuff left over to open another coal mine from scratch! Another observation I made on these regular mooching missions was when I went for a mooch around in the stores and workshops, I found lots of craftsmen's personal lockers still padlocked up and stuffed full of brand new tools and possessions that had been hoarded and so religiously guarded over the years, and now all these once precious things were all destined to go to the scrap yard!

A typical example of this hoarding and which was particularly personal to me, was when I went for a mooch in my in old Chock fitters workshop where I used to be deployed from at the start of every shift. On entering the first thing I noticed was that the big grey cabinet locker that used to stand behind the boss's office desk was still there in place, not only that it was still locked from the day it was last used. To confirm if it had anything inside I gave the locker a nudge with my shoulder and it was very heavy, which was a good indication it was still full of stuff and especially exciting to me, because this locker and its contents was always safely guarded by our boss, which he made all too obvious each time he went inside to get something out, because he only ever opened the door slightly ajar to prevent anyone else seeing what he kept inside, so it was always a mystery to us what was actually in there.

In those days whenever myself or anyone else in the Chock fitting team had lost or had broken a tool (which was more often than not our most essential tool the Bacho Adjustable spanner) he would automatically tell us there wasn't any available at the mine, although we knew he had some stashed in his locker, it often resulted in the chock fitter in question having to replace the tool at his own cost. He was a right tight fisted twat, he was more bothered about saving the colliery a petty amount of money than whether his men had the right tools for the job, and all the while he had this penny pinching attitude our senior management at the area headquarters were flying around in helicopters from one banquet to the next.

So as one can imagine I was especially excited to see what was inside and I couldn't wait to get it open to see what booty may lie within. I swiftly opened it using my universal key and when its double doors sprang open wide I was gobsmacked to see this hoard of brand new shiny things, pliers and Stilson Wrenches, Allen Keys and the biggest prize of all, there was box full of about ten pair of each of the three sizes of Bacho adjustable spanners that we all regularly used and had to beg for!

In the tail end of my career at Sharlston I became the acting charge hand of the Chock department on the afternoon shift for a short spell, and in that time I would often make good use of the Blacksmiths' workshop to carry out equipment repairs, but also for making the odd items for home. The foreman of the Blacksmiths was called Ken and he was a smashing bloke, he would help me out with anything I was doing, unlike other workshops foremen who didn't like outsiders coming into their space, Ken was more obliging and happy to help me out, but to be truthful I think he just liked to laugh at me trying to arc weld, especially when I kept getting caught out by the electric arc flashes that burnt the retinas of the eye, usually resulting in me having sore eyes for a few days. (A flash felt like having sand in your eyes for about two days).

So on my next mooch I headed to my old haunt the Blacksmiths' workshop just to have one a last look around before it was all gone, and here again I found everything was still pretty much the same as it was left, and despite the fact a couple of bits of machinery and a Blacksmith forge had been removed, it all still looked quite the same as I remembered it. But once again it was an eerie sight to see all the men's lockers now wide open, and still with all their owners' personal pictures and memories pinned inside of the doors. Tools were still laying where they were last put and Overalls and clothing were strewn all over the floor, resembling a finite and uncaring departure, just like it was the last day of school, and the old clock that I had checked so many times before still hung on the very same office wall.

After I had finished mooching around, I took the time to sit quietly on an old work bench to reflect on all the memories I had in there, but also to try to absorb some of the left over energies of those bygone days, by just sitting with my eyes closed with a clear head. In the short time I was there I began to hear voices and definite sounds of someone walking about. As I listened those noises got closer and louder, at first they were coming from the next workshop, but then I could hear the footsteps close by, then all of a sudden I heard a loud crash that made me jump and it startled me a bit, which sounded exactly like a spanner had been thrown to the floor and it was only just feet from where I was sat, on hearing this my eyes sprang wide open and for some reason that day I lost my nerve, which is something I have never done before, and instead of sticking around to find out what it was, I shot out of that building faster than a robber leaving a bank!

Which brings me onto my final ghost story? This sighting occurred at Nostel Colliery where the company had employed a night watchman to guard the pit top overnight to stop thieves and to prevent nosey people or kids falling down the shafts that were now open and not fenced off. On one particular morning of the watchman's shift we had just arrived at the colliery entrance in the minibus that I was driving, and on turning into the colliery lane but still about 50 metres away from the perimeter fencing of the site, stood this night watchman who looked to be in a state of alarm, so I pulled up the minibus and wound down the window to ask what was a matter, to which he bleated like a scared little boy. "I'm not going back in there," he said, and on hearing this my boss jumped out the van to question this bloke, and now everyone in the van was listening to this conversation as the night watchman went on to tell his story.

He said he had gone into this old cabin and he was having a cup of tea, he swore he hadn't nodded off to sleep, but he was just sat back relaxing when all of a sudden this hooded Monk walked into the cabin and sat down beside him! He then said he froze and just stared at this Monk, but when this Monk looked like it was turning its head to look at him, he jumped up from this bench and belted it down the road as quick as he could, also adding that he had actually been stood on the outer perimeter for five hours on his own waiting for us to come on site!

I believed his story for two reasons, 1: He lived in the Barnsley area and he wouldn't have known it had been part of a Monastery, 2: He refused to go back to work there, and because he was set on solely to do the job of a night watchman the company had no choice but to lay him off! (We couldn't wait to tell his replacement though, haha)

The actual shaft filling was easy, a Chute was centralised over the hole which was fed by conveyor and the rubble was loaded onto that by mechanical shovel. The only strenuous thing I had to do was at the end of the day's fill and that was to lower a weighted cable plumb bob to the top pile of the fill and measure the length of the cable to calculate the depth filled compared to square meter of rubble that went down, this was to ensure that the shaft walls hadn't collapsed and bridged the fill which could leave cavities that might sink at a later date! They had constructed a drum like a fishing reel that had a manual handle and when we first started filling the shaft it was really hard winding this thing up and down the depth of each pit shaft, and by the time I had wound up a couple of thousand feet of cable and the plum bob weight, my biceps, triceps, shoulders and stomach ached so much it felt like I had just done a full upper body workout in the gym.

Day after day I wound that drum of cable up and down the same Birkwood pit shaft that I had ridden in a cage thousands of times before, until eventually and weeks later the rubble fill finally peaked at the top of this once deep man made hole in the Earth. Which should have been a bit of a poignant moment for me, but before I had any chance to dwell on the matter my mate interrupted any sentimental moment I might have had by instantly daring me to jump on the top pile, and teasing me by saying "That if I was so cock sure it was fully compacted and I was confident it was done correctly, I shouldn't have any fear of doing so"

In order to show him I wasn't afraid I quickly jumped onto the fill without any hesitation, although I have to admit it was a bit unnerving, but I managed to mask over any nerves I had by mimicking the famous Walter Houston dance that he did in the film *The Treasure of the Sierra Madre* when he found gold!

However, no sooner had I run out of wind through acting the fool trying to make my mate laugh, and just as I was trying to get my breath back, I was suddenly overcome with an emotional realisation that seemed to come right through my feet and straight up and in to my head, of all those memories that were made down that hole in the ground, which were now entombed in that dark place that will never see a man or hear a voice ever again, and as those memories flashed through my mind I was suddenly consumed by not only a sense of sadness, but also one of guilt.

On the Scrap Heap

It was around the end of this contract when I received my final discharge from the physiotherapy centre at the local hospital and it was then that I was advised by the orthopaedic surgeon that it wouldn't be good a idea for me to go back into the mining industry, which he explained was due to the fact I had too many breaks in my leg and the plates and pins needed to stay in place, and because they did, he said that if my leg was to ever suffer any more trauma or get hit by a rock again, it was a possibility I could lose it!

On top of the leg problems though, I was now getting severe back pain, so the while I was at the hospital I told the orthopaedic surgeon about it, and he insisted on me having an x-ray to find out what was causing the pain. After the x-ray plates came back they clearly showed that my bottom vertebra of my spine was hanging off half an inch out of its place, to which the orthopaedic consultant remarked that it was either caused by a defect from birth or I had been in a very bad car accident in past. But I hadn't been in a car accident, and when I put it to this consultant that I had indeed been in a very bad train accident and asked if that could have been the cause, he said it definitely could have been, but it would be very hard to prove!

On the hospital's advice I reluctantly had to tell the mining company that I couldn't return back to my old job and as far as any type of labouring work was concerned it was completely out of the question and I had finished with the mining industry. On me giving them the notice I was no longer any use to them, they then gave me the notice they were laying me off, which wasn't too surprising considering their line of work.

These were worrying times, not only had I lost a really good well paid job, but it now looked like I was losing my physical ability to gain any livelihood at all, which was a bitter pill to swallow because I had always been an active person both in work and in fitness sports. Although it was bad news at first I remained optimistic that things would work out in the end. But my back pain grew worse by the day, it got so severe it eventually restricted me from doing any type of work at all, my feet would go numb and sometimes I actually lost control of my bladder, and that's when my alarm bells really started to ring, which instigated me to go and find out if anything could be done, as a result this orthopaedic surgeon then advised me to wear a steel banded corset for support, and when I asked him how long a period of time I had to wear it, he told me that I would have to wear it for the rest of my life!

The trouble was that this corset only made my back worse because it allowed the muscles in my back to weaken, as a consequence of this draconian method of treatment it nearly crippled me and as a result I was unable to work for quite a number of years.

Fortunately years later by the way of a more modern approach, new methods were introduced into physiotherapy that did away with the old traditional way of thinking and the use of corsets and supports and suchlike and encouraged exercise to build muscle strength instead. Only after a short while of this treatment my back improved greatly and although it did it wasn't quite 100% yet, I still had some trapped nerve problems, which meant that some days I was ok and some days I wasn't, therefore I was unable to assume any position for long without discomfort.

That is until the day I discovered the one thing I couldn't get on the NHS and that was a Chiropractor. On my first visit the Chiropractor noticed that I my spine was actually out of line and after some light manipulation he managed straightened me up again. After that session my lower back as been a lot better and although I still have to make the odd return visit to keep my spine straight, this was the only treatment that enabled me to return back into the workplace again (Which begs the question, why don't the NHS provide this treatment?)

My next line of work though, was far more dangerous than working in any coal mine, but that was another chapter in my life story which I have no doubt will fill as many pages as this in my next book!

And it is on that note I would like to close this book, but not before making this one last statement

Yup, they were Dirty Days alright and dirty for more reasons than the book's title might first suggest, although they were and despite having more spills than thrills and all the hardships we all had to endure, I still can only look back with fond memories of all the good times we all had together, and I would like to say that it was an absolute privilege to have been able to work alongside some of the finest men in the country, but on top of that it was an absolute honour to have been able to stand shoulder to shoulder with those Lions of men who stood on the picket lines in the epic struggle of 1984, which as indeed created an everlasting bond between us all that only a 100% striking miner knows.

Admission: To be honest, if someone was to ask me today if I was proud to be a miner, I would answer yes, but only for the couple of reasons stated above, I'm certainly not ashamed to have been a miner. If they were to ask me, do I regret my choice of work, I would have to say no, it was the choice I made. But if they were to also ask, if I had a choice to start all over again would I have still gone down the pit, I would have to honestly say, no — would I bollocks!

P.S. At the start of my book I happened to mention that my life is full of weird experiences, so I think it only fair to prove that point by telling you the weirdest tale of them all.

Many years ago when I was about 15 yrs old I managed to get a date with a beautiful young blonde haired girl who I had been wanting to date for ages, she looked a bit like Dolly Parton to me and she had similar size chest, but better looking! On my first date we walked down the carriage drive in the Newland area and I was hoping to have a bit of a kiss and cuddle at the end of our hand in hand stroll. Unfortunately we accidentally bumped into my old crew (gang).There was about thirty of them in all and they were all heading towards the Calder river, but they were all carrying sticks and they also had a big fierce dog with them. It turned out they had organised a pre-arranged fight with the East Moor lot because of an altercation the day before at the sand quarry where we all used to swim, and they were going to straighten things out once and for all! Normally I would have been at the forefront of this situation, but seeing as I had this gorgeous young lady with me I felt I had much better things to do at the time, so we parted company with the Normy faction and then we went looking for a nice cosy place to sit for a while ... Haha. Yet all the while we were kissing and cuddling and trying to get my hands up her shirt, all we could hear was this massive commotion coming from the opposite side of the river, to which I had no choice but to investigate, after all they were mates that I hung about with. On crossing the river and nearing where all the shouting was coming from we both saw that the East Moor lot was on one side of the river and the Normy lot on the other, and at this point they were merely shouting obscenities and daring each other to cross the river to have a fight, which was quiet harmless at first, it was like two dogs barking at each other from opposite sides of a gate, and it probably wouldn't have come to much. Me and my Dolly Parton girl friend were mere spectators and we were laughing at how funny the situation was, that is until the East Moor contingent suddenly produced some air rifles and they began shooting at us, and my date actually got shot in the middle of her back with a pellet! This action made by them left us no choice now but to cross over the bridge with the intention of kicking their heads in, and by the time we reached the other side I was now leading from the front and was practically frothing at the mouth furious. But when we went over the railway crossing to get to the field the East Moor lot where, a load of police suddenly appeared on the scene and they came running down the hill towards us with their dogs on long leads, which made both sides scatter and leg it. Unfortunately my bird and a few stragglers got caught and as a consequence of them blabbing our names to the police, about sixty of us ended up in court. (It was no surprise either that Dolly Parton packed me after that incident) Those of us who pleaded not guilty at a later hearing got off with a small fine for trespassing on British Rail property even though we wasn't trespassing (magistrates could get away with things like that in those days, come to think of it they still do!).

A few years later I was stood in a shop doorway sheltering out of the rain while waiting for the 5.15 am paddy bus to Sharlston colliery, when this new starter came and stood in the same doorway with me. This young man was also called Pete and we were about the same age,the first thing he noticed was that I was wearing my Stranglers badge on my leather jacket, it was an enamel one with the silhouette of a rat crossing a setting Sun lit background which featured on their *Rattus Norvegicus* album, to which he happened to mentioned that he liked them a lot and he had seen them play live, and because I had also seen them a few times myself and they were my favourite band we started to get on like a house on fire. It wasn't long before we became really close mates, but the weirdest thing was that when I got to know him better, it turned out he was one of the East Moor lads that shot my Dolly Parton date and he said he got sent to a borstal for it. We laughed about it when we realised who was who, a good job really because he ended becoming the best man at my wedding!

The CO OP matchbox signed by Arthur Scargill was actually his, and the only reason I ended up with it is because Pete gave it to me to save and since he had passed away. God bless rest in peace!

Match box story

Myself and Pete and his brother Jerry once attended a miners Gala at Thornes park in Wakefield in the late 70s and all three of us had been drinking in the famous beers tents. Later in the afternoon we were a bit drunk and we began acting around and play fighting, and for some reason Pete wanted me to help him take his brother's trousers off to leave him walking around with no pants on (as you do) but Jerry was a big lad, so it was going to be a struggle. There we where wrestling around in this straw that had been put down for some reason? When were suddenly approached by Arthur Scargill, who just happened to be walking across the park on his own, at first he had a look of concern on his face because he thought that we were actually fighting, but he laughed when we told him what we was doing. Pete was thrilled to meet him and more than delighted to shake his hand. On introduction Arthur asked Pete what he did down the pit, and when Pete told him that he was only a button man, Arthur immediately rose from his heels and began to lecture him, but to build him up also, when he said "You're not just a button man, you are a transfer point attendant and an integral part in the production of coal and you are no less important than the man on the coal face or the colliery manager, don't you ever forget that!" he said practically jabbing is point home with his fore finger into Pete's chest. After hearing this uplifting appraisal we all shook Arthur's hand and thanked him, and after Pete got his signature we parted company. Pete, who was around the same height as me walked around like he was 7 ft tall for the rest of the day. So nice one Arthur Scargill!

And it wouldn't be fair to finish without telling of the nicest experience I ever had while working underground.

I was working in the middle of the coal face early one morning on the day shift, and although I knew my wife was heavily pregnant with our second child and she was very near to having it, we both reckoned he wasn't coming yet. There I was working away and frantically trying to get this front canopy leg of a hydraulic chock fitted before shearer needed to get by, and no sooner the canopy was up and the chock was fixed and set in place, the shearer was already passing underneath the canopy I had just set. So it was a close shave and I was quite exhausted, but even before I could rest up I heard my name being shouted on the tannoys system once again, but it wasn't calls of "Chock fitter wanted" this time it was by name and it was from surface control! "PETE MCGOWAN YOU'RE URGENTLY REQUIRED AT HOME, YOUR WIFE'S WATERS HAVE BROKEN, AND YOU'RE NEEDED AT HOME STRAIGHT AWAY!" And all over tannoy system for everyone to hear too! On hearing this it instigated a massive shout out from everyone on the district, even from some that were listening in out-bye. The main gate end men got ready to stop the face chain in the gate, allowing me to ride on the coal to get me off the face quicker, and once in the gate I jumped straight on a conveyor that was kept clear of coal for me to ride on to make my way out-bye. Everyone I passed on that journey were cheering and when I had arrived at the lifting station the staff had even organised a diesel locomotive for me to ride me back to the pit bottom, and no sooner I landed there, they had already stopped coaling purposely to put the gates back on the cage so I could get home. Everyone was just brilliant; it makes me proud to this day thinking about it. The funny thing was that when I went crashing into the house half expecting to hear lots of moans and groans and excitement, but instead my wife was just casually sat at the dining table and busily chatting away to our good neighbour supping tea! She had him a few hours later though.

Thanks for reading!

THE END